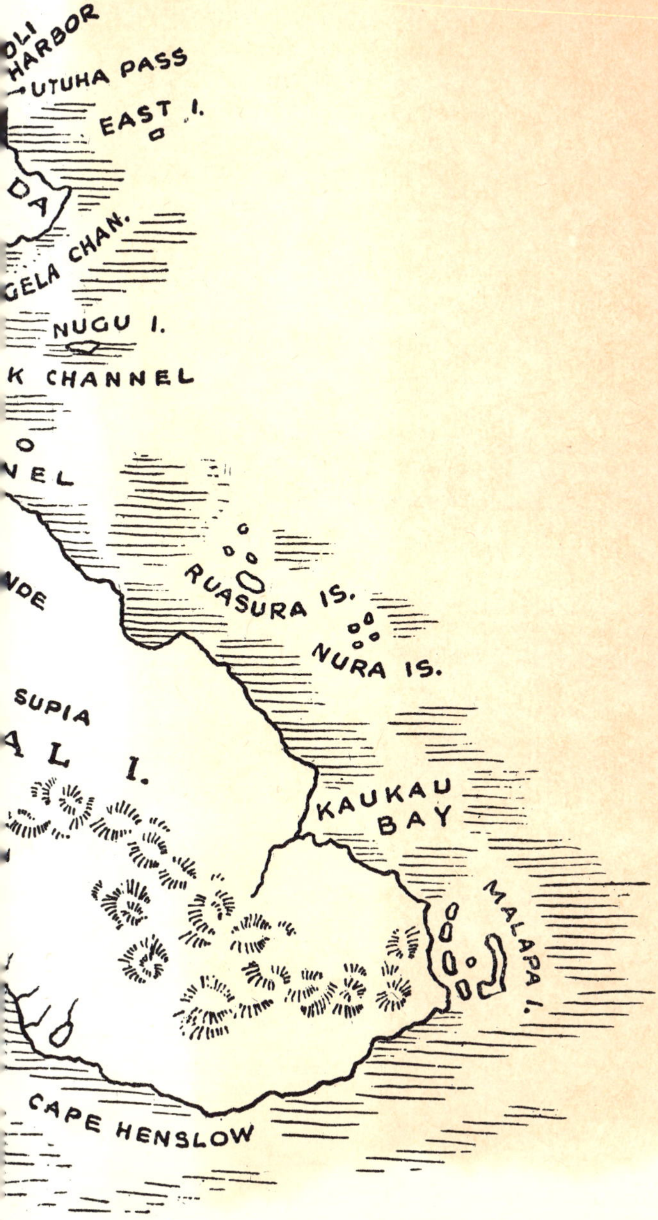

OLI
HARBOR
UTUHA PASS
EAST I.
DA
GELA CHAN.
NUGU I.
K CHANNEL
O
NEL
RUASURA IS.
NDE
NURA IS.
SUPIA
AL I.
KAUKAU
BAY
MALAPA I.
CAPE HENSLOW

LONG WERE THE NIGHTS

*THE SAGA OF A PT BOAT SQUADRON
IN WORLD WAR II*

LONG WERE THE NIGHTS

THE SAGA OF A PT BOAT SQUADRON IN WORLD WAR II

by

HUGH B. CAVE

WITH THE COOPERATION OF LIEUTENANT COMMANDER ALAN R. MONTGOMERY, U.S.N., LIEUTENANT ROBERT L. SEARLES, U.S.N.R., AND LIEUTENANT (JG) LEONARD A. NIKOLORIC, U.S.N.R.

Illustrated by EDWARD L. COOPER

ZENGER PUBLISHING CO., INC.
P.O. BOX 9883 ● WASHINGTON, D.C. 20015

COPYRIGHT, 1943
BY DODD, MEAD AND COMPANY, INC.
COPYRIGHT RENEWED 1971 BY HUGH B. CAVE
REPRINTED 1980
BY ARRANGEMENT WITH
DODD, MEAD AND COMPANY, INC.

ALL RIGHTS RESERVED
NO PART OF THIS BOOK MAY BE REPRODUCED IN ANY FORM
WITHOUT PERMISSION IN WRITING FROM THE PUBLISHER

This edition is an exact unabridged reprint of the original 1943 edition, and also contains photographs and drawings which were not present in the original edition.

Frontispiece photo courtesy of J.M. Searles

ISBN 089201-091-6
LC 79-67545

PRINTED IN THE UNITED STATES OF AMERICA

TO THE OFFICERS AND ESPECIALLY THE MEN OF SQUADRON "X," AND ABOVE ALL TO THOSE WHO ARE STILL OUT THERE FACING THE ENEMY.

PUBLISHER'S NOTE TO THE NEW EDITION

BECAUSE of wartime security restrictions existing at the time this book was originally published, it was necessary to refer to the PT boat squadron which is the subject of this narrative as Squadron "X", and other squadrons as Squadron "R", etc. Since these restrictions no longer apply, it can now be noted that Squadron "X" was actually Squadron 3(2), while Squadron "R" was really Squadron 2, and Squadron "T" was in fact Squadron 6.

Foreword

"I LIKE to think," said Squadron Commander Montgomery, "we gave the Japs something to remember. I like to believe we helped even the score for the PT men who fought so magnificently in the Philippines. And we were lucky. We were not expended."

He lit a cigarette and relaxed a little behind his desk in the PT Shakedown Office. Alert, slightly built, with an easy smile and the brightest of bright eyes, 38-year-old Lieutenant Commander Alan R. Montgomery has the look of a man who seldom remembers to do much relaxing. He hails from Warrenton, Virginia. Out of Annapolis, 1927, he is Navy to the soles of his sea-boots. Here in Miami, where I talked with him and two of his Squadron "X" boat captains, and learned from them what happened in the Solomons, the commander is hard at work training new men for the mosquito fleet.

It is important that new men be trained for the mosquito boats, because the little PTs have proved their worth now in offensive action and will be increasingly valuable as the war continues.

"We were lucky," said Alan Montgomery gently. "We were but eight small boats, eighty men and a base force, assigned to what you might call the 'Night Shift' against a sizeable part of the enemy's South Pacific Fleet. The odds

FOREWORD

against us were slightly terrific, I suppose. But we didn't go out there with any idea of being pushed around. The PT boats are designed to face such odds."

He is right about that. The Patrol Torpedo Boats, though small, pack a punch all out of proportion to their midget dimensions. Seventy-seven feet long and made mostly of plywood, they carry two pairs of vicious fifty-caliber machine-guns in turrets at the sides of the cockpit, a twenty-millimeter machine-gun aft, and four torpedo tubes whose snouts are aimed forward at a slight offset so that the "fish," when fired, will clear the curving edge of the deck. All the machine-guns can be used against airplanes as well as surface ships, and, when submarine hunting, the boats can be fitted with depth charges.

No attempt has been made by our navy to glamorize the little thunder boats. They are not even named, but are designated by numbers. Built without an ounce of armor and loaded to the teeth with lightning, they are literally high-speed projectiles stripped to the barest fundamentals and afraid of nothing under, on, or over the sea.

The crew's quarters, under the forward deck, are just big enough to hold four double bunks. The galley is a hot-plate in a niche. The cockpit, so-called, is merely that portion of the deck abaft the windshield, where officers stand at wheel and throttles. The after deck is a cat-walk between gun turrets and torpedo tubes. The engine-room is a crowded, fume-filled, thunderous little hell-hole beneath the after deck where the engineers have just enough head-

FOREWORD

room to keep their knees straight, and the three Packard airplane engines grind out the power to send the little boat hurtling forward at a speed of fifty knots or more.

Each boat is manned by a boat captain, his executive officer, and a crew of eight, all of whom are thoroughly trained for torpedo boat work and despite the rigors of their existence are fanatically proud of their boats and their jobs. There are no finer men in the navy.

"Especially," said Commander Montgomery, "the enlisted men. That's why I say we did not go out there with any idea of being shoved around. We had a great gang of boys. Really great. We had been training rigorously for months, going through all the motions, putting ourselves and our boats through every conceivable kind of shakedown, and hearing all those tantalizing reports of action so far away that it seemed in another world. Every man in the outfit was itching for a poke at the real, live thing."

"Sure," said Lieutenant Robert L. Searles, with a grin. "Oh, sure." Bob has a nice grin. An easy, confident grin. He is twenty-three, a good-looking, finely built boy from Leonia, N.J., and a graduate of Princeton. And while you listen to him, you watch his grin and know very clearly what he means. He sat on a desk in the commander's office, his legs dangling.

"The real, live thing," Bob said. "Oh, sure. We had some times, too. But you know the biggest thing we did? I'll tell you. We were the fellows who brought the sandman to the Marines on Guadalcanal. We delivered sleep. Those

FOREWORD

ships we sank—those little Jap flags we painted on our PT emblem over the doorway in Sesapi—they were not nearly so important as the sleep we delivered when the Marines needed rest more than anything else on earth." He looked out the window at the blue of Biscayne Bay and said, "I mean that," and was not grinning. "Ask Nick," he said.

Lieutenant (jg) Leonard A. Nikoloric, a quiet, dark-haired boy from Englewood, N.J., looked at me and nodded. Nick is a Princeton man, too—the same age as Bob. Phi Beta Kappa. And has been called a hero—which he is, and which he doesn't like.

He has a good memory. You know it by the gravity of his expression, by his sometimes reluctant smile and the way he has of looking at you without exactly seeing you.

"Four months," Nick said, "is a long time. Especially toward the end."

You know what he means. It is not so very far from Tulagi, in the Solomons, to this peaceful office in Miami. You sense, looking at Nick and Bob and Monty, that they can shut their eyes and be back there very quickly, remembering the long, dark nights, the insects and heat, the big and small dangers that made up four months of fighting.

They remember, too, the gentler things: the red-dog games and the Charlie Chaplin movie, the squadron's pet kitten, the string of foxholes in the wake of Doc Perkins. And most of all they remember, and cherish, the friendship of the men who fought with them. For a PT boat is small.

[x]

FOREWORD

Its crew is a combat team. No one man is more important than another.

Not all of Squadron "X" came back. Illness took its toll. Some are still out there. But in four months of swift and savage action, the squadron lost not a man or a boat to the enemy, despite the Japs' most ambitious efforts to liquidate them. And the line of little Jap flags on the PT emblem at Sesapi was long indeed.

This, then, is the story of eight motor torpedo boats and the men who manned them. If, in the pages that follow, some of these men appear more often than others, it is only because the three who told the story remembered more of what happened on their own boats than on the others. That is only natural. But Squadron "X"—the entire squadron—is the story's hero.

H. B. C.

LONG WERE THE NIGHTS

THE SAGA OF A PT BOAT SQUADRON IN WORLD WAR II

Chapter One

Stand by with eight Motor Torpedo Boats for action somewhere to the westward.

Such were the orders received by Montgomery in the summer of 1942, at the Panama base where his midget mosquito boats were stationed. A short time later in the dog days of August, cargo ships arrived to take the first four PTs and their equipment out. Squadron "X" was thus officially born.

Neither Montgomery nor his men knew where they were going. They had hunches, yes. Not a man among them, looking at a map, could resist the impulse to look longest and hardest at the South Pacific. But this was August. Guadalcanal and Tulagi were in the headlines, but were not yet names of magic dimensions. The Marines had landed to contest those troublesome patches of island jungle with the Japs, but the future was shrouded in Pacific fog.

Montgomery's men had no time for conjecture in any case. When the cargo ships arrived, officers and men worked night and day, almost without rest, stowing aboard stores and ammunition. The boats were cradled and loaded. On the twenty-ninth day of August, the first four boats said good-by to Panama. The remaining four, in charge of Lieutenant Hugh M. Robinson, Squadron Executive Officer, were to follow shortly.

LONG WERE THE NIGHTS

Almost, but not quite, Squadron Commander Montgomery waved his farewells from shore instead of from the deck of an outbound ship. He had not felt too chipper those last few days of frenzied activity. The heat, perhaps. Or the lack of rest. Or a touch of "something-or-other." Panama in August is acrawl with something-or-others by which a man can be laid low very quickly. A touch of fever, a dizzy feeling, a sudden bewildering realization that you are not hot any more but cold and shivering, and you are down for the count.

Monty was down. It was a ticklish interlude. His men, frantically concerned, hovered around him as anxiously as kids suddenly sobered by the illness of a beloved parent.

But they need not have worried. Squadron "X" was not being pushed around, not even then. Advised to give up his trip to the fighting zone in exchange for a comfortable bed in hospital, Montgomery would have none of it. The trip and the ocean air would put him right back on his feet, he insisted. When the unit sailed, he sailed with it.

Two days later he was under treatment, without further protest, for pneumonia. "But I honestly thought," he insisted to Bob Searles at the time, "it was Panama Flu."

Says Searles, his grin eloquent: "He honestly thought we believed him."

"I was flat on my back, reviling my luck," Montgomery recalls with a wistful smile, "until we arrived at a South Pacific base. Our PTs were assigned to the command of

LONG WERE THE NIGHTS

Admiral Kelley Turner, Commander of Amphibious Forces in the South Pacific, and I was told to make all necessary preparations to be towed to our destination.

"The preparations took time. Equipment at the base was not what it might have been, and we had the devil's own job getting our boats into the water. PTs are small and made mostly of plywood, it's true, but they pack a lot of weight below decks and you can't just pick them up and walk off with them. Lieutenant 'Rosie' Ryan had a leg broken. Another man was cracked on the head by a boom. A dozen were beautifully black and blue.

"We got the job done, however, and then the boats were fueled and camouflaged, painted dark green so as to be as nearly invisible as possible against the jungle backgrounds of the region for which we were bound. The machinist's mates gave their engines a final going-over. Golden, Long and Tufts rechecked the equipment. Nothing was overlooked.

"The men really babied those boats. For one thing, these PTs were not the gorgeous new craft that some people seem to think they were. They had been in service almost a year and differed little in design from the boats in which Bulkeley and his men fought so valiantly in the Philippines.

"And we really loved the boats," Monty recalls. "I don't think I'm a sentimental sort, but there is something about a motor torpedo boat—maybe its size, or lack of size—that makes it very human. When you have lived with one, nursed it, teased it to best behavior and cussed its frequent temper

LONG WERE THE NIGHTS

tantrums, you reach a frame of mind where, if that little 77-foot sliver of plywood and punching power were suddenly to wink an eye and talk to you, you wouldn't be too surprised.

"Another thing: the boats were home to us. We weren't back in Panama now. We were on the prowl, separated for God knows how long from wives and sweethearts. The boats were all we had—four small boats for forty men. Don't get me wrong. I'm not sentimental. You wouldn't call any of us sentimental. But you feel those things all the same. They're important."

The first contingent of Squadron "X" left the base on the sixth of October. It was a bright, breezy morning, a travel-folder morning. Out of the little port, destination still unrevealed, steamed a converted yacht and a cargo ship, stern and gray in their war paint. The yacht, skippered by Lieutenant Commander Charles B. Beasley, was to be the PTs' tender.

Beasley was having his troubles, too. Much of the equipment he so sorely needed was back in the States, where indifference and shrugged shoulders had been the answer to his frantic requests for cooperation. "Hell," he'd been told, "you're not going anywhere. We need that stuff for a real warship."

As a matter of record, the yacht was the first and for a long time the only ship of any size to be based in the explosive fighting zone to which the PTs were going. Other ships sneaked in, unloaded with all possible haste, and fled out to safer regions. Beasley stayed.

At the start, the trip was placid enough, but before it ended it was rough indeed. High winds pushed up a sea through which the cargo ship lumbered with decks awash and the PTs' tender had to fight for headway. The tiny mosquito boats bobbed and skittered like bits of paper on a kite-tail.

Tow-lines parted with annoying frequency. When they snapped, the PTs had to roar ahead under their own power to hook on again. In those heaving seas it was dangerous work.

"One man who won't ever forget that delightful trip," says Bob Searles, "is 'Wiz' Wisdom—torpedoman Hobert Wisdom—who was riding the boat, skippered by Stilly Taylor. The PT was behind the cargo ship and those waves would lift her out of the water with a terrific wallop. Time and again the line let go, and Wiz had to go overboard at the forefoot to make it fast again.

"He had a dozen hands, that boy, and knew exactly how to use them all. Wiz had been in the navy a long time and was the biggest man on Taylor's boat, in fact one of the biggest in the outfit. He was tough as nails and knew his business.

"He'd hang on with four or five of those hands of his and yell instructions to the bridge, while Stilly worked him closer and closer to the cargo ship. One mistake on Stilly's part in handling the wheel, and Wiz would have been pulverized.

"Well, he'd work down there with that balky tow-line under conditions that would have left a less rugged man white and shaking. The waves beat him half to death and every heave of the bow added to his bruises. But Wiz had his own cure for the shakes. He kept up a running harangue at everyone in sight. He bawled hell out of them all, includ-Stilly and exec Stan Thomas, and colored his barrage with the most gorgeous sea-going grousing you ever heard. It was an education to listen to him.

"Then, the job finished, Wiz would climb back on deck and shove his fists into his hips and growl, 'Goddam it, that's too much. That's the last time I'll ever do a thing like that. Goddam it, I'm through!'

"He was a wonderful and amazing guy, that Wisdom. Without him we'd be there yet."

On the morning of October 10, drenched and weary from four days of pounding by high seas and violent winds, Squadron "X" reached another South Sea base. The men were still officially unaware of their ultimate destination but secretly certain now that they were bound for the string of lady-finger islands to the northwest—the Solomons—where American and Jap forces were trading blows with increasing animosity on land and sea.

"At this base," says Montgomery, "I received orders

LONG WERE THE NIGHTS

to fuel to capacity at once and be ready to leave on a moment's notice. When the men heard that, they knew we were in.

"We worked like beavers. We had come a long way and done a lot of wondering about where we were going and what we'd be getting into; and now we were close. There was action just over the horizon. We were due to see some of it soon. Perhaps you have some idea of what that meant. Pearl Harbor, Bataan—we thought of all those things. A little, anyway. And of the months of preparation. But the biggest indication of how we felt was the way the men dived into their duffels in search of letters from the folks back home—old letters, already read and re-read, which now became very important.

"But first, of course, we had to get there. That posed something of a problem."

It was more than "something of a problem." It was a ticklish bit of business that had to be worked out with extreme attention to the matter of timing.

The four PT boats were to be towed out of the base by a pair of old DMSs—four-stacker destroyers which had seen action in World War I. The delicate part of the plan was to arrive before dark at a point from which the mosquito boats could cut loose under their own power and, by roaring through the night at top speed, make their destination before daylight—and before they ran out of fuel.

If the PTs did not reach their goal before daylight—if,

that is, dawn found them still at sea with any considerable distance still to be covered—there was the very excellent chance that Jap planes, on patrol, would spot them and put them out of business. For the Japs had control of the air. Only above Guadalcanal, where Marine fighters could rise to dispute them, were they meeting sufficient opposition to make them cautious.

Moreover, there was the element of surprise to be considered. Montgomery's men now knew where they were going. Their base was to be Tulagi, a tiny island occupied by Marines on August 7 as part of the same operation which established American forces on Guadalcanal. They knew, too, the nature of the particular job they were to do. It was to put a stop, if possible, to the nightly shelling of Guadalcanal by Jap ships which slipped down from Bougainville —the "Bougainville Express"—and were depriving the Marines on Guadalcanal of sleep.

Surprise, therefore, was a potent weapon not to be lightly risked. If the PTs could reach Tulagi and hole up without being spotted, their first nocturnal sortie against the enemy would come as a bolt from the black, catching him completely off guard.

"If you'll study the map for a moment," Montgomery points out, "you'll get a clear idea of the situation there. Our Marines held part of Guadalcanal and all of Tulagi. The channel between, about twenty miles wide, was no man's land. Running up to the northwest is a double chain of islands—Santa Isabel and Choiseul on the east, the Russell and New Georgia Islands on the west. At the top of that tube sits Bougainville, on which the Japs were solidly entrenched.

"Night after night, with all the gall in the world, the Japs had been pouring down from their Bougainville base. They knew—and they knew the Marines knew—that the dark nights belonged almost exclusively to them. Those Marine pilots on Guadalcanal could not go out in the dark to hunt them down, nor were there any shore guns on the island big enough to touch them. And the Japs were always mighty careful to be out of there, well out of range, by daylight.

"If we could put a stop to that, or even scare them into being a little less brazen about it, the situation would be improved. Remember, our Marines had been on Guad since August 7. From the beginning, Jap Mitsubishis had been over in daylight, raining bombs on them, and Jap troops had been doggedly trying to squeeze them out of their little strip of land around Henderson Field. All day every day they ducked bombs and fought Japs. Then at night, when they wanted sleep, these Jap destroyers and cruisers would slip down through 'the slot' to pour explosives into them, driving them into foxholes.

"We were going to try to stop that. Somebody had to. Marine airmen were making the Mitsubishis pay dearly for the daylight bombings, and from the bloody battles at the Tenaru, the Matanikau and Lunga Ridge, the Japs on Guadalcanal were learning that the job of pushing our troops back into the sea was going to call for reinforcements . . .

but the task of winning some sleep for those men was ours.

"And speaking of reinforcements," Montgomery continues, "we had work to do there, as well. The Bougainville Express was doing more than just keeping our Marines in foxholes all night. It was getting Jap troops ashore with disturbing regularity. The enemy had about given up trying to do that by daylight—his losses were too great in the face of our air protection—but at night he managed to get his men onto the island, a few here, a few there, and the Jap strength on Guad was continually being bolstered by these men who sneaked ashore under cover of darkness.

"Our job was to stop that, too. Otherwise, with typical Jap tenacity, the enemy would keep on reinforcing his strength on the island until our sleepless Marines were whittled down and eliminated. So with a man-sized job ahead of us, we were counting heavily on that element of surprise. When the Japs did learn of our presence, we wanted to be very sure they found it out from *us*.

"That's why, when we cast off from our escorting four-stackers just before dark on the evening of October 11, we were all pretty tense and worried. And as things turned out, we had good reason to be."

When the lines were cast off, the PTs were on their own. Montgomery as squadron commander chose to ride the boat captained by Bob's brother, Jack (Lieutenant John Malcolm Searles of Leonia, N.J. and Princeton). One PT was captained by Lieutenant Henry S. "Stilly" Taylor of

LONG WERE THE NIGHTS

Cold Spring Harbor, Long Island—a tall young man who went to Yale and, as an amateur yachtsman, had cut himself a sizeable reputation on the waters of Long Island Sound. At the wheel of another was Bob Searles. Another boat was skippered by Lieutenant Thomas Kendall, a slightly built, capable boy from Minneapolis. Bob Wark (Lieutenant Robert C. Wark of Portland, Oregon), this boat's regular captain, had been flown in to Tulagi ahead of the boats, to make preliminary arrangements.

Plans were complete. Every man was on the alert. Now at top speed the four thunder-bugs roared farewell to their escort and raced for their destination.

For Montgomery and his men this was strange territory. Their charts, of course, had been memorized. The shape and name, if it had a name, of every knob of land were fixed firmly in their minds from long hours of map study. But it was a weirdly wonderful world after all.

The night was dark but not quite black. A pale wash of starlight dimly polished the smooth sea and silvered the comet-tails of phosphorus in the boats' wakes. Out of the dark, odd shapes took form with perilous swiftness if they were near, or with tantalizing slowness if large and distant. At forty-five knots, in waters renowned for the inaccuracies of their charting, anything could happen. It was a little like driving at breakneck speed along an unlighted country road at night, not knowing when a fallen tree might block the way or a bridge might be out.

"It was also," says Monty wryly, "a little like swimming

in strange water that just might be full of sharks—which was the prospect we faced if anything went wrong with our calculations."

Toward morning, as the boats rounded the eastern end of Guadalcanal Island and swung into Lengo Channel, the monotony of racing at full throttle through tricky darkness was suddenly shattered. Ahead, lightning flashed and thunder rolled. But the lightning was a quick, bright burst of gunfire; the thunder was a rumble of naval guns near Savo Island, the sound echoing back and forth along the dark peaks of Guadalcanal and Florida.

"We slowed our speed," Montgomery reports, "and looked the situation over—what we could see of it. Obviously our navy and the Japs were having some sort of altercation near Savo. It might be a minor action, a quick trading of blows in the dark, or it might be something big.

"In either case, there was a strong possibility the Japs would come pouring out of the eastern end of the channel and meet us head on. That was bad. We were nearing the end of our run, remember, and fuel was dangerously low. Moreover, we were loaded with extra equipment and had a lot of the base force personnel aboard. If the Japs did turn into us, we'd be in the unenviable position of a man trying to fight with his feet tied and his arms full of bundles.

"We went ahead slowly, with our fingers crossed, every man ready to jump into action at a second's notice. And we were jittery."

But the Japs did not come. The rumble of gun-thunder

LONG WERE THE NIGHTS

grew faint, and the four PTs were soon speeding on course again. Later they were to learn that they had come within a few minutes of being an impromptu part of the Battle of Cape Esperance, in which units of the United States Fleet surprised a Jap landing operation and sent the enemy reeling back to the northward with the loss of a cruiser, four destroyers and a transport.

Dawn was half an hour distant when the boats reached Tulagi. Their margin of safety in regard to fuel had been almost as slim.

Remarked Dutch Ebersberger, machinist's mate, a stocky, muscular lad with a hearty sense of humor: "We got plenty of gas. Almost enough to clean a midget's pants, if he was a nice, tidy midget. What, for Pete's sake, were we worried about?" He turned to Happy Parker. He and Parker, also a machinist's mate, were always riding each other, always together.

Said Parker dryly: "Maybe you'd like to do it over again."

They could laugh then. The tension of the run was over. But the night's ordeal had told on every man in the outfit. All were exhausted, dirty, soaked with sweat and salt water.

"Silent Joe" Nemec, who was to succumb later to an attack of peritonitis, looked around wistfully and said with a laugh—Joe never raised his voice: "If only we had some nice, feather-lined foxholes now, that a fellow could stretch out in for a couple of weeks." But there was no time for foxholes. Before daylight came with its threat of Jap bombers, the PTs had to be holed up and hidden.

LONG WERE THE NIGHTS

Paced by chief boatswain's mate Charlie Tufts, who seemed to be everywhere, the men worked their arms nearly off in the next few hours. First they had to scout the shores of Tulagi for suitable hiding places: up tiny jungle creeks, in the shelter of winding inlets, under sprawling mangroves whose roots reached down through iridescent salt water and clung like octopus arms to the coral bottom. Then the boats had to be hidden, serviced, readied again for action, and carefully smothered under canopies of camouflage. The Japs, who winged daily out of the north in their big, fast bombers to strike at Henderson Field, sometimes paid Tulagi a visit en route. And they were smart.

"All that day," says Montgomery, "the men worked. They were dead on their feet and ready to drop, but there simply was no time for rest. As Squadron Commander, I went up to Marine headquarters to report to General Rupertus (Brg. Gen. William H. Rupertus of Washington, D.C.) and then rode a utility boat over to Guadalcanal, to report to General Vandegrift (Maj. Gen. Alexander A. Vandegrift of Lynchburg, Va.) who was in command there. It didn't take long for word to get around among the troops on Guadalcanal that I was a PT man, and the reception I got was really wonderful. I suddenly was surrounded by hundreds of friends I'd never met before!

"I like to think, of course, that this was because our boys were PT men. Perhaps that was it. Certainly those Marines didn't have to be told why we'd come and what we were going to try to do for them. But perhaps the reason for the

LONG WERE THE NIGHTS

reception I got goes deeper.

"Remember, those boys had been taking all the Japs could send at them since August 7, without reprieve. When they found out that our squadron, or half squadron, of motor torpedo boats had come in to work with them, they may have felt that here at last was recognition, however small, for the job they'd done. They hadn't been forgotten after all.

"But mostly," Montgomery recalls, "they were thinking of those damned Jap ships that slipped down the slot at night to shell them. They had an amazing string of unprintable names for that nocturnal annoyance, and were counting on us to do something about it. I remember one haggard, red-eyed youngster who came up to me with a Jap knife stuck in his belt and said, 'Just teach the bastards to stay home in bed nights where they belong. Just do that, and we'll remember you in our prayers.'

"I hoped we could do it."

That evening, after a day spent in smoothing out plans for action, Montgomery flew back to Tulagi in "The Duck" —a utility plane maintained by the Marines for liaison work and shuttle service between the islands. The PTs were shipshape, and the commander spent the rest of the evening at Marine headquarters on Tulagi, working out problems of communication and cooperation. The men, meanwhile, were industriously setting up a base.

It was quite a base. Located in Sesapi, a village once occupied by natives (and before the coming of the Japs, by a few whites also) it consisted principally of a broken down marine railway and a few sad shacks.

The railway was worthless. The shacks were little more than upright poles capped with Vs of thatch and populated profusely by a wonderful assortment of bugs. Nevertheless, it was home.

The native shacks were reinforced and put to various uses, one converted into a storehouse, another into the squadron office. While work was progressing on the latter, Harold "Johnny" Johnson, a quartermaster, came forward with a PT emblem—the famous "fighting mosquito" emblem designed by Walt Disney. These had been removed from the boats when the battle zone was reached, because even at night they shone gloriously and made most enticing targets.

Johnny proudly climbed up on a box of replacement parts and nailed the fighting mosquito over the squadron office doorway. Squadron "X" had arrived. It was now official.

Said machinist's mate Winter, a tough little guy whose dual hobbies were kidding his officers and borrowing their money: "Well, this is it. Bring on your Japs."

Chapter Two

SQUADRON "X" had arrived at Tulagi the morning of October 12. A little more than thirty-six hours later the boats were in action.

"We got word the afternoon of the thirteenth," Montgomery says, "that a Jap task force was 'in the slot' and moving down toward us. Apparently it consisted of three destroyers, or a cruiser and two destroyers. Patrol planes had spotted them and the word was passed along to us.

"When I heard it, I went at once to General Rupertus to find out what he thought about it. I told him I didn't consider it wise to sacrifice our number one weapon of surprise on so small an enemy. No fooling—that's what I told him. It will give you some idea of what we thought of those boats of ours.

"The general agreed that we should wait for something really worth while. He smiled as he said it. Now that I look back on that little conversation, I realize why he was smiling; but at the time, there was nothing very droll to me in the idea of four midget PT boats haughtily refusing to attack a trio of Jap destroyers because the Japs weren't big enough.

"We stood by, out of hiding and ready for whatever might develop. The men were nervous and eager, going through all the emotional tension of a fighter about to step into the ring for his first bout. In his mind, each was undoubtedly reviewing the hundred and one things he had been taught, wondering if, when enemy guns began thundering, he would come up to scratch. I was wondering myself."

Soon after midnight, guns began a booming conversation in the vale of ink between Tulagi and Guadalcanal—that restless stretch of sea called "Sleepless Lagoon" by the harassed Marines. The guns were big ones and the conversation was one-sided. The island remained silent. Down from Cape Esperance toward Lunga Point, Jap ships moved swiftly in close formation, hurling their heaviest shells at Henderson Field and the Guadalcanal shore.

Obviously the enemy had schemed up something more than loss of sleep for the Marines this night. An operation of considerable magnitude was in the making.

"I ordered all boats to get under way immediately," Monty says, "and sent word to General Rupertus that 'this was it' and we were going out."

With engines muffled, the four PTs slipped quietly out of Tulagi harbor and headed for the gunfire across the channel. It was a black night, tar black; there was no moon at all, and thick low clouds concealed the stars. But over there off the Guadalcanal shore the darkness was punctured by those bright, bursting balls of fire from Jap guns, and by the gaudy, graceful loops of color hung in the sky by tracers.

The PTs deployed, moving in four abreast, feeling their

LONG WERE THE NIGHTS

way forward through the dark. A motor torpedo boat is not an angry bull, thundering to the attack at top speed. It is a marauding cat, belly down, employing stealth and silence.

"We moved in," Monty says, "with little more noise than a whisper. I was aboard a boat, conning for Jack Searles, and we were slightly in the lead. On our left were Bob Searles, Bill Kreiner and their crew. On our right were the PT with Stilly Taylor, Stan Thomas and their men, and the PT with Bob Wark, Tom Kendall and gang. The men breathed slowly and deeply to steady their nerves. No one spoke unless it was necessary. This, at last, was what we had come for.

"Clearing Tulagi harbor there were the four of us, and at first we maintained contact with one another. That didn't last long, however. In the dark we soon lost touch, and you had a feeling of aloneness that sat in your throat like an egg.

"As a rule, of course, darkness is our ally. But this time we had those blinding flashes of gunfire to contend with, nearer now every minute, and it was hell. If only they had let up long enough for us to adjust our eyes—but they didn't. Our eyes never did get adjusted.

"It was like being stabbed continually in a dark room by a powerful searchlight. You'd blink at the glare and feel the brightness of it eating into your head. You could almost feel a kind of physical pain. Then the darkness would come pouring back, deeper and more solid than before . . . and all the time, of course, there was the deafening thunder of

LONG WERE THE NIGHTS

the Jap guns, rolling out through the night until it was caught up by the islands and kept alive in echoes.

"And then, closing, we made out our targets. There were four of them. Big ones. Three were cruisers and the other was almost certainly a battleship.

"It was about that time, on Stilly Taylor's boat," Monty recalls with a chuckle, "that machinist's mate Tubby Kiefer made the classic remark for which he was kidded ever after. Spotting the nearest of those four Jap monsters, Kiefer turned excitedly to gunner's mate Teddy Kuharski and said in a hoarse whisper: 'Gee, Ski! Ain't that the *Boise?*'

"It was not the *Boise*. No, indeed."

Searles' PT continued closing, her engines still muffled. She had selected the last Jap in line for her target and was close, almost close enough. Behind the plexiglass windshield, Jack Searles kept a nervous hand on the throttles, with Monty beside him. Radioman Lester Piper, a quiet, soft-spoken boy who became leather-tough in a fight, crouched in the cockpit with the radio phones hot against his head, maintaining contact with Cavanah, Purvis and Stephenson on the other boats. Quartermaster "Johnny" Johnson stood ready at Piper's side.

The set-up was perfect. In another moment the torpedoes would slip from their tubes, the boat would turn and make its dash for safety with throttles wide open. Nothing to it. That essential maneuver of PT tactics—the silent approach, the swift surprise attack, the racing retirement

LONG WERE THE NIGHTS

—had been run off a score of times in practice. Every man knew every wrinkle of it.

But the boat had performed another maneuver of which her crew was altogether in ignorance. In the dark she had slipped past a force of Jap destroyers without even knowing they were there.

The other boats were less lucky, and suddenly the night became violent.

Two boats had run not through the screening destroyers, but straight into them. Jap searchlights came on, sweeping the sea. The PTs were spotted.

Bob Wark swung his wheel hard over and at full throttle ran from the rain of shells that reached for him through the dazzling lanes of light. The move was almost fatal. The lights had momentarily blinded both Wark and Tom Kendall, the boat's exec, who stood at Wark's elbow. Now from the brilliant glare they roared into darkness again, and were on top of a second Jap destroyer before they saw it.

Torpedoman "Danny" O'Daniel sent up a banshee yell. The men instinctively ducked. Only Wark's quick reaction, swift as the click of a camera shutter, saved the PT from head-on collision.

He turned the boat just in time. "If I'd had a swab," said quartermaster Ralph Crumpton later, with a shudder, "I could have painted my name on that Jap's side. Boy, we were close enough to see the guys on her gun platforms and hear them holler!"

But the Jap was quick, too. His searchlights came on and his machine guns began an angry chatter. Luckily his main batteries were out of it; the PT was so close aboard that he could not depress the big guns to train them on her. But the machine-gun fire was vicious.

Todd and Blackwood, the gunners, braced themselves in their turrets and returned the enemy's fire. They had never been under fire before, these boys. This was their baptism. But they knew their guns and their job. The mosquito boat's powerful fifties poured a blistering answer at the Jap, raked his bridge and searchlight platform, shot out his lights. Todd was later commended by Admiral Halsey for his fine shooting that night.

With machinist's mates Cline, Nelson and Long teasing every ounce of speed from her engines, the PT sped on into darkness, free from pursuit.

Stilly Taylor's boat was running, too. Enemy destroyers had pinned her in their searchlights and were hot after her —two of them—firing 4.7s and machine-guns. It looked bad.

Torpedoman Wisdom was not grousing now, or if so it was under his breath. Machinist's mates Peterson and Barnard were not indulging their favorite pastime of kidding each other. Ship's cook Henry Bracy, famous for the succulence of his pies, was not thinking of new ways to tickle the boys' palates. The two destroyers were gaining. The

LONG WERE THE NIGHTS

night was so full of enemy ships that the PT could find no room for running.

"Smoke!" Stilly yelled. "Make smoke!"

Quartermaster Boyd Kleinworth relayed the command in louder and lustier language. Wisdom, frozen by an after torpedo tube, dropped his mallet and jumped to the smoke generator. In a moment a dense white cloud was pouring out astern. Stilly gripped the wheel, facing ahead to find a lane of escape through the crowded night. Stan Thomas, at his side, spoke softly, reporting the action astern. The ten men on the PT had been trained as a team. They were a team.

With the Japs fumbling in the smoke, the boat zigzagged through the dark and neatly gave them the slip. Then at full speed she headed out past Savo Island—not to retire, but to try for the prey she had hoped for in the first place: the cruisers and the battle-wagon.

Meanwhile, Bob Searles and his men were having themselves a time. "When the hell broke loose," says Bob, "we were some little distance from the other boats. How it happened I don't know—in the dark it's almost a wonder we were there at all. Anyway, when Stilly, Bob Wark and Monty ran into trouble, we were half way across Sealark Channel. Almost at the same instant, trouble caught up with *us*.

"Lights suddenly came on," Bob recalls, "and there, dead ahead, was a Jap destroyer. Remember, we hadn't known there were any destroyers in this task force—only cruisers and a battleship. This one was as surprised as we were, and we had time to turn and run for it. Torpedoman Scottie Lueckert was aft on the smoke apparatus, and we soon had a lovely, billowing blanket of white smoke to hide behind.

"The Jap must have thought we were parked there like a sitting duck, because he poured shell after shell into the smoke without coming close to us. So . . . we decided to get him.

"We turned and went for him, but just then saw Bob Wark off to starboard. He was apparently having difficulties. His gunners were swapping fire with a Jap who was much too close for comfort. We ran over to give him a hand.

"Just what happened then I don't quite know, nor did Edwards, Mehes and the other boys when I asked them later. There was confusion everywhere. All those Jap destroyers—there were eight of them, we found out afterward—were rushing around trying to protect their big ships, and the four PTs were darting in and out like wasps, fighting to get through the destroyers and close the cruisers. It was a little like an old-fashioned Fourth of July. You'd hear a roar, and one of our boys would come boiling out of the dark and go by you. There'd be a flash of light, a burst of thunder, and a Jap shell would rip up a big, wet chunk of ocean, usually too damned close.

"Anyway," continues Bob, "we started over to see what we could do for Wark, and suddenly a big, beautiful target loomed up in front of us. We had closed a cruiser on her way back up the line to Bougainville.

"It was a set-up. The PT sped for position and at four hundred yards fired her after two torpedoes. One cleared the tube, struck the edge of the deck and went in. The other didn't.

"Now a torpedo is a complicated and temperamental piece of mechanism. It is fired by an electrical impulse charge, which sends it singing from the tube. At that point the torpedo is a dead fish and wouldn't explode—at least in theory—if you hit it with a sledge-hammer. But as it travels through the water, the sea winds up a set of fins in the war-head and cocks it, about the way you'd turn the blades of an electric fan by aiming a jet of air at them. After the fish is cocked, or 'armed,' a seven-pound blow on the nose is sufficient to explode it.

"This one stuck in the tube, and when that happens a lot of other things can happen. The fish is 'working'—its internal mechanism has been set in motion and its propellers are whirring, and running full blast out of water like that, with nothing to cool it, it may get red hot and weld itself to the tube. If the sea is rough enough to smother it with spray while the boat is making knots, the spray may wind up those fins in the war-head and cock it, and then—boom.

"So there we were," Bob recalls, "with that torpedo having a hot run in the tube, and our attack incomplete. I don't like to remember it. The only calm man on the boat, I'm sure, was quartermaster Meadows, who was big and burly and never lost his head. But I can't say for sure that even he was calm then, because I was too jumpy myself to know what anyone else was doing.

"The fish in the tube was making a terrible racket, like a car tearing along with a broken connecting-rod. And we were closing the cruiser. She was only two hundred yards ahead, and we were going on in.

"Meadows fired the other two torpedoes, and one of those stuck, too! Then we made our turn and got out of there like the well known bat out of hell—so close that we passed the stern of the cruiser with less than a hundred yards of clearance. She could have blown us sky-high with a hit from one of her big guns, and at that range I can't see how she missed. Her 20-mms. were spouting away at us like Roman candles. We were lucky.

"And suddenly we were jubilant. Because, as we ran for it and dodged those pesky twenties, a terrific explosion tore the Jap open forward. Another followed almost instantly. We could feel the concussion, the pressure and suction in the air. The Jap stopped firing at us.

"We made for our base then. Our torpedoes were gone, except the two stuck in the tubes, and there was no point in hanging around. Bill Kreiner took the wheel and I went below to see if things were shipshape. Down there I found machinist's mate Lorran Beed, one of the sweetest engineers in the outfit, calmly and methodically checking the engines, just as though nothing had happened. Winter and Nemec worked by his side.

LONG WERE THE NIGHTS

" 'Everything all right, sir?' Beed asked quietly.

"I said it seemed to be.

" 'That's fine,' he replied. He was always quiet like that, always polite. I don't think I ever heard him swear. When he talked, it was usually about his wife and children back in Brooklyn.

" 'I think we hit a cruiser,' I said.

"He rubbed his oily hands together quite gently and said that was good, very good—and went back to his engines.

"We made for the base slowly, with an eye on those fish half out of the tubes."

Jack Searles' boat was the only one of the four to slip through the destroyer screen without being seen. When the night erupted behind her she was closing her target, the last cruiser in line, and was about five hundred yards off the Jap's bow. The Jap was alert, aware of danger. His lights came on, sweeping the sea. But the PT had not yet been spotted.

She went in another hundred yards, lined up her sights and fired two torpedoes. That was all she had, the other two having been removed to make space for depth charges. Moving at sneak-in speed with engines muffled—the perfect approach—she sent those two torpedoes winging.

Momentarily the boat slowed to allow the fish to clear her. Then she came about and with throttles wide open for the first time, raced for cover. Behind her the night burst into flame as a torpedo hit the mark.

LONG WERE THE NIGHTS

"And right there," says Montgomery wryly, "we got the surprise of our sweet young lives. We had been running wide open for just about two seconds when Jack Searles, who was always thinking of his engines, said ever so casually, 'We can slow down now, Commander. They didn't spot us,'—and he eased back on the throttles.

"I didn't have a chance to answer him. A salvo of enemy fire burst around our ears, and we were damn' near blown off the boat! Jack and I both jammed the throttles wide, practically up through the windshield, and the PT went soaring. What had happened—in turning from the cruiser we had run smack into the whole hornet's nest of destroyers and were neck-deep in trouble before you could say 'Jap!'

"Remember," Monty continues, "we had slipped through this destroyer screen without seeing them, and didn't know they existed. We had an idea something was up when the other PTs went into action, of course, but were too busy with our cruiser to pay much attention. Now we were suddenly caught in searchlight beams and were trapped there between the Jap capital ships and their escort, with the destroyers pounding us.

"Everybody ducked. Later we all got a good laugh out of that, because, of course, there is nothing on a PT boat to duck behind. The cockpit may look comfortingly solid, but is built of ⅜ inch plywood that would hardly stop a good sneeze. But this was our first time under fire and we were really catching hell, so we ducked.

"As we took off at top speed in the general direction of

LONG WERE THE NIGHTS

Tulagi, there were two destroyers on our tail and they were determined to get us. Enemy shells, mostly 4.7s, screamed around us like rockets, and the gun flashes were so continuous that they lit the whole place up like daylight.

"A Jap 4.7 is no toy. It very nearly equals the five-inchers on some of our own warships. You hear a screaming whistle, then a shell goes winging overhead with a sudden sharp crack like a pistol shot, and you see a section of sea leap skyward. And all the time you feel the quick, sharp bite of the gun flashes against your eyeballs, eating right into your head.

"We were seeing plenty of those flashes and dodging plenty of Jap shells."

The PT was winging, but the Japs had the range on her. Their shells came closer. One explosion smothered the fleeing boat with spray and forced her to use every evasive maneuver in the book. Lunging, weaving, throwing herself from side to side, the little boat fought for freedom.

"Make smoke!" Monty shouted.

Torpedoman Willie Uhl, quietly efficient, had been waiting for that. He had quit his place at the tubes and was already over the smoke generator. The white stuff poured out and a Jap shell burst in the midst of it, squarely in the boat's boiling wake. Uhl was thrown to the deck.

He got up again, uninjured. He was tough. The others were tough, too. They were not ducking behind plywood now. In the engine-room, chief machinist's mate Ramsdell, usually a very cheerful guy but now grim and all business, worked like a termite to keep the three Packard 4Ms humming. In the 50-caliber turrets, Happy Parker and ship's cook Carideo, whose duties in action embraced more than cooking, were ready on the guns and begging the skipper to let them cut loose. Aft, on the 20-mm., Dutch Ebersberger had the foremost Jap in his sights and was waiting.

The order to fire was not given. The Jap was doing well enough as it was, without presenting him a clear-cut target at which to aim. It hurt. It was a sin and a shame. But the PT's guns remained silent.

The leading Jap was in the smoke now, hunting his prey, but the smoke was thick and the shells he poured into and through it went wide. "We could see his tracers," says Monty, "streaking by us—small red balls of fire, some of which seemed to hang suspended in space for an incredibly long time as they passed us. Those Japs were good gunners but couldn't locate us, nor could they see where the shells were falling. Without smoke we would have been done ducks for certain."

But now the two destroyers were in the thick of the smoke and the Japs knew they were close. They began using machine-guns, spraying the night ahead of them with a rain of bullets. Jack Searles swung the PT wide, and Montgomery turned to shout an order.

"Depth charges! Drop the ash-cans!"

"The idea seemed worth trying," the commander recalls, "and fortunately it worked. Johnson, Uhl and gunner's mate

LONG WERE THE NIGHTS

Osborne dumped the depth charges overside so fast it was almost comical—yet when you stop to think of it, such coordination was not comical at all, but remarkable in a gang of boys who had never before found themselves under fire. "The cans were well astern of us when they exploded. We saw the columns of water go up—swift, climbing towers of spray, very close to the Japs—and the concussions jarred the deck under us.

"We hardly hoped to damage the pursuing destroyers. That would have been sheer luck, and too much to expect. But we did hope it would confuse them, perhaps cause them to think they'd run into a mine field. And apparently that's what they did think, because when the cans went off, the Japs at once ceased firing."

The PT was making knots then, Ramsdell souping her engines for all they would take. The Japs laid back astern and appeared to be cautious. Elated, Montgomery ordered the smoke pot overside, where it would continue to make smoke and might fool the now nervous enemy into thinking the elusive PT had gone down.

Uhl and Osborne heaved it over. In the machine-gun turrets, Carideo and Parker sighed their disappointment and relaxed. They hadn't fired a shot. Nor had Ebersberger, on the 20-mm. With engines trimmed and muffled, the boat slipped in close to the murky shore of Florida Island.

"Looking back," says Monty, "we could see the Japs nosing around the spot where we had jettisoned the smoke generator, and I suppose those monkeys were excitedly telling one another we were done for. They hovered around the smoke for quite a while, perhaps waiting for what was left of us to come up. When they'd gone, we got under way again.

"Our plan was to slip around Florida and hole up in the first safe hiding-place until daylight, when the Japs would go home. It seemed the wisest thing to do, because Sleepless Lagoon was full of Japs and any attempt to go through them, back to our Tulagi base, might be suicidal.

"So at slow speed, ghosting along with every man alert for more trouble, we felt our way past the Florida shore—and suddenly found the way blocked by a destroyer lying to across Sandfly Passage. Apparently he was doing sentry work for the force which had come steaming into the channel.

"There we were, and there he was, and the only thing we could do was cut our engines, sit tight, and send up a fervent, ten-man prayer that he would not discover our presence. Our retreat was cut off by the Japs astern, who were still sniffing around the smoke."

Those were bad moments and long ones. The PT could not attack. She sat weaponless, with the unsuspecting Jap looming large and lovely, dead ahead. It was discouraging. A single torpedo would have blown the "Jape" to hell, and there was all the time in the world to wish him there. But the PT's torpedoes had been expended on the cruiser. Fluently but softly the men cursed their luck.

LONG WERE THE NIGHTS

Before dawn the Japs departed. It was safe then to head for home.

"We started our engines," Monty remembers, "and discovered to our complete disgust that we were stuck fast. The bottom there was of coral, wickedly sharp, and the ebbing tide had dropped us on a reef. We couldn't move.

"Jack, Happy, Dutch and some of the others went overside for a look and found we were hard aground. Then, as the tide went out still more, the coral began to punch holes in our light plywood bottom, and we began to fill. There was nothing to do but wait for aid. For us, the battle was over."

It was over for the other PT boats as well. Bob Searles, having eluded pursuit, was lying to off Tulagi harbor, and with daylight went on in. Wark, after his brush with the Japs, had swung back into the thick of things and tried again and again to press home his attack on the battleship and cruisers. But the big ships had not lingered. With the mosquito boats driving at them from all quarters, they had ceased firing, darkened ship and fled out of there, not knowing what manner of foe they had encountered. In the dark the boat was unable to locate them and spent the remainder of the night scouring the waters between Guadalcanal and Tulagi, all hands fighting mad and vainly praying for a shot at something.

It was much the same with Stilly Taylor. Shaking the destroyers, he had raced out past Savo at top speed to try

LONG WERE THE NIGHTS

for the big ones. But at daylight Stilly and his crew were still plowing up the waters of Sleepless Lagoon, hunting in vain for a target. At dawn the two boats came on in.

What had Squadron "X" accomplished? Four of them had attacked a Jap force of one battleship, three cruisers, eight destroyers. That was the official tabulation. One boat had scored a hit on a cruiser. So had the two others, and Bob Wark's boat had probably killed some Japs with their machine-guns. Was that all?

Not quite, though the men were bitterly disappointed at the time and could not see beyond it. What they *had* done was to disorganize an enemy force of twelve warships, causing it to abandon its mission, turn tail and run. Four little thunder boats had done that. It was an achievement.

Psychologically they had done more. They had hit the Jap with a new and frightening weapon, putting the fear of God into him. He would be less brazen the next time. He would think twice before sending his heavy stuff into an area so packed with peril.

The cruisers? "We sank one," says Bob Searles. "Who did it we don't know, but she went down with all hands. We found it out next day, when reconnaissance reports came in."

There was a postscript to that battle. Chief radioman Layton supplied it, a couple of days later, when he emerged from the base radio shack wearing a broad grin and waving a bit of paper.

LONG WERE THE NIGHTS

"Message," he said, "from Tojo, relayed from Australia." The men crowded around. What they read was a Jap communiqué covering the action in which Squadron "X" had met its baptism of fire. It was as follows:

"Seven of our ships engaged nineteen motor torpedo boats during which twelve motor torpedo boats were destroyed and incidentally one of our cruisers was sunk."

Just incidentally.

Chapter Three

Jack Searles' boat was stuck fast on the coral reef.

"At low tide we could see what we were up against," Montgomery says, "and it was heart-breaking. The coral was chewing at her bottom and there was not a chance in the world of getting her off without assistance. It was like standing by a friend with a broken back, watching him suffer.

"Piper had radioed the base for assistance, and now there was nothing to do but wait for it to arrive. There was danger, too. The boat was a perfect target for any Jap pilot who might discover her."

To kill time, the men explored the beach. But the proper vacation spirit was lacking. Happy Parker and Dutch Ebersberger were not riding each other. Ramsdell could find nothing now to be cheerful about. They discussed the previous night's action and wondered about the cruiser they had stalked. Some were sure she'd been hit. Said old-timer Johnson impatiently: "I *know* we hit her. I saw it."

They hoped he was right.

Before long they had company. Osborne and Piper, walking the beach together, saw a movement at the jungle's edge and stopped in their tracks, alert for trouble. But the fuzzy-haired native who popped his head out was not looking for trouble; he was just curious. Presently he advanced, followed

LONG WERE THE NIGHTS

by others.

They were a sorry lot, these Solomon Islanders. Shamefully mistreated by the Japs, they had fled into hiding back in the hills and were still too terrified to show themselves when American Marines arrived in August. Only lately had they been moving down from their jungle hideouts, a few at a time, to reoccupy their abandoned villages.

They were black, jet black, with mops of bushy hair. Their teeth were bad. Many were deformed. A few of the younger bucks, with matrimonial aspirations, had dyed their hair red to show they were on the make.

Willie Uhl tried to talk to them, employing what he proudly believed to be pidgin English. Surprisingly they understood him, or seemed to. But their own pidgin English was another tongue altogether, and after a struggle to make sense out of it, Willie had to give up.

The others tried. Said Piper to one of the red-thatched bucks: "Mebbeso you got fellers back village come chop-chop give us hand with go-boat, huh?"

"Hell, that's Chinese," said Carideo.

"Shut up. He knows what I'm sayin'. Don't you, Handsome?"

Red-thatch grinned. His teeth were stumps.

"See?" Piper said. "You watch now!"

The native beckoned to his comrades. They went down the beach to the boat and stood around admiring it, jabbering as excitedly as the red and white parrots in the jungle. Then they went away.

LONG WERE THE NIGHTS

They didn't come back.

Toward noon, Jap bombers came over. There were many of them, on their way to give Henderson Field a workout. The sky was black with them.

"It was a tense moment," says Monty. "We knew they could see us. The boat was sitting there big as life, and there was nothing we could do to conceal it. We stood around looking up, machine-guns ready, expecting any moment to see one or two of the buzzards swoop down to blow the boat to bits.

"Piper, ordinarily a quiet boy, began growling under a curled upper lip. Tough Johnny Johnson had his fists clenched and was calling the Japs a string of long, loud names. Jack Searles looked worried.

"But the Apes ignored us. They're peculiar that way. They saw us—couldn't help but see us—but your Japs have one-track minds. Once their plans are laid, they stick to their assignments. This time their assignment was to bomb Henderson Field, and they flew right on over us.

"When we told the boys on Tulagi about it later, they said they knew. They'd heard our sighs of relief clear over there at the base."

That afternoon a yippie chugged in. They were rugged little boats, the YPs stationed at Guadalcanal and Tulagi. Originally California fishermen, members of the tuna fleet, they had been commissioned by the navy at the start of the

LONG WERE THE NIGHTS

war and dispatched to the fighting zones to perform whatever tasks were required of them. The skipper of this one was a big, bull-throated man who believed in getting his work done in a hurry.

"I wish I could remember his name," Monty says, still amazed at the man's energy. "He was a character, that fellow, going to win the war all by himself, without a damn for anyone or anything. Later we saw more of him, and the things he did with that boat of his were incredible.

"It was a dumpy little tub, beamy and battle-scarred, but he'd go anywhere at all in it with complete disdain for danger. 'Japs?' he'd say disgustedly, as though discussing a few harmless mosquitoes. '*Japs?* Why, them little sawed-off squirts!' He was marvelous, really. In no time at all he had us off the reef and back at the base."

But the PT was in bad shape, out of commission with her bottom full of holes, and replacement parts were not available. Some had been brought in on the boats, but the heavier stuff was aboard the PTs' tender, which had not shown up yet. For the time being, Jack Searles and his crew were without a boat.

They were an unhappy lot. Not even a meal of special Marine Corps beans and the knowledge that Squadron "X" had sunk a cruiser the night before could bolster their spirits.

On the morning of the fifteenth, in daylight, the enemy struck at Guadalcanal again. It was not the Insomnia Express this time but a fleet of troop-laden transports escorted by a battleship, some cruisers, and a formidable armada of destroyers.

Planes from Guadalcanal met them in the slot and sent one or two of the transports to the bottom. The rest of the invasion fleet determinedly came on. PT Squadron "X" stood by awaiting orders, and was told to sit tight.

"It was probably best," says Monty. "With Jack Searles' boat out of commission and Bob Searles' boat having trouble with her torpedo tubes, we had only two craft available. Besides, this was a daylight set-to, and our little thunder boats were never meant to go roaring into an enemy force of that size in daylight. We'd have been expended out there and knew it, and we had to save our boats to keep Tojo busy at night. If we lost them, the Japs would have had the run of the place again. So we hurried up to our lookout post on the bluff behind Sesapi and watched the action through high-powered binoculars.

"It was quite a show. Our side was on the short end of the deal that day, because of a lucky hit the Japs had scored the night before on some navy dive-bombers at Henderson Field. Only eight of the bombers could be patched up to fly that morning, and here was a good part of the Jap fleet steaming in to put troops ashore.

"Well, it was amazing. Those eight remaining planes took off from Henderson Field in relays, two at a time. They winged out over the Japs and through a blanket of AA fire that filled the whole sky with exploding clouds of smoke. Then they'd peel off, one after the other, and go screaming down at the transports. It was the transports they were after —the ships loaded with troops.

"I wish you could get the picture, because to us it was the greatest show on earth. When we weren't holding our breath in a paralysis of astonishment, we were cheering ourselves hoarse.

"The Japs were firing everything they could lay their hands on. It seemed as though every gun on every one of those twenty or more ships was trying to out-bellow the others. And our planes, two at a time, would go tearing through the stuff as though it simply didn't exist.

"Nearly every bomb was a hit. It had to be, because the boys in the bombers were diving headlong at the transports. We thought some of them would plummet straight down the ships' stacks. It was tremendous.

"After a while the Japs gave up for a time. They were taking too much punishment and had to retire, leaving some of their number behind. But the show went on.

"Off Kokumbona, three of the transports were ablaze from bow to stern, exploding like bundles of firecrackers. There'd be a terrific eruption, hurling a dense black column of smoke into the sky. Then the smoke would move away on the wind and the ship which had exploded would still be sitting there, apparently unharmed except for little rivers of fire running red along her deck. Then another explosion, another billowing geyser of smoke, and the same thing all over again.

"Those ships blew up time after time before they sank,

and when they did go down they settled very slowly, bow and stern together, holding up their masts like hands. They're still there, resting upright on the bottom with their superstructure above the surface. Later on, when the Japs on Guadalcanal were starving and were calling the place 'Death Island,' those gutted ships must have seemed to them very symbolic of something.

"The enemy was not through, though. He was hard to convince. Retiring, he reassembled his forces and steamed in for another try at landing his troops. This time the ships encountered B-17s which had come racing up from one of our bases to the south, and those army bombers and the planes from Guadalcanal hit them as a team. It was just too bad.

"They landed some troops—about 15,000 according to reports we heard later—but not one of their transports got away, and many went down with all aboard. The few that attempted to escape were sunk as they fled. How many Japs were drowned for every man who was put ashore, it's hard to say. From Tojo's viewpoint, far too many, certainly.

"But the thing that impressed us most, as we watched from our lookout post, was the incredible daring of those dive-bomber pilots. It gave us a tremendous lift and made us very humble."

The Japs had put some troops ashore, but had been able to land few supplies and little in the way of equipment. That brought Squadron "X" back into the picture. For the enemy had to equip and supply his men in order to make them effective, and would undoubtedly attempt to do so at night. For the PTs, this meant patrol work.

"We hardly looked forward to it," says Bob Searles. "Our boats pack their biggest punch when employed as a team, each crew functioning in close coordination with the others. Patrol duty meant that we would have to go our separate ways and work as independents. But it had to be done, so we worked out a system of beats to cover Sealark and Lengo Channels, Cape Esperance, and the Guadalcanal shore.

"But first," Bob recalls with a sly grin for Montgomery's benefit, "there was a little job to do for the men on Guadalcanal. Just a minor chore, not worth mentioning, really. The skipper was there and can tell you about it."

"I was there, all right," Monty admits wryly. "We were ordered to escort the island's two yippies over to Guadalcanal with a load of supplies urgently needed by the men there. It looked like a routine job and no one wanted it. Stilly Taylor and Bob Wark were elected, and I rode along with Bob, mostly for the ride.

"It was dark and we expected to get word at any moment that the Express was on the way down, but we managed to get over there with the yippies, crawling along at eight knots, without incident. A couple of lighters were waiting in the shadow of Lunga Point to unload the supplies. Nobody else was around except Pistol Pete.

"Pistol Pete, as you know if you've been reading the

newspapers, was a Jap gun, a five-incher or something about that size, which had been pestering the Marines on the island for a long time. Marine pilots had been trying for days to locate him but couldn't because he was so well hidden.

"He'd thrust his snout up, lob a couple of shells in the general direction of Henderson Field or the Marine encampment, and then duck down again under cover before anyone could put the bee on him. He was a nuisance, but the damage he did was slight.

"Tonight, however, Pete had moved. He was nicely established in new quarters on a hill from which he could lob his shells off Lunga Point—and he'd been lobbing them at the lighters. And now that we had arrived with the supplies, the boys on the lighters were in a big hurry to get the job done and be out of there.

"In the dark the unloading was difficult, but of course we couldn't show a light. Then to add to our troubles the sea began to kick up, and before we could do a thing to prevent it, one of the yippies had snagged herself on a reef.

"There we were," Monty recalls, "the yippie hard aground and the Express almost certain to be on its way down from Bougainville. Fortunately most of the supplies were then aboard the lighters, and they were able to clear out. That helped. But what to do with the grounded YP boat?

"I suppose we should have left her there and escorted the other one back to Tulagi. If it had happened a few weeks later, we probably would have done just that without hesi-

LONG WERE THE NIGHTS

tating. But we were new to this business, remember, and were terribly reluctant to take a licking. And as it happened, the grounded boat was the one which had pulled Jack's boat out of a similar situation just a while ago. We owed her something. Anyway, we stayed.

"With the tow-lines out we went to work—all in the dark, remember, and it was so dismal, inky dark you had to be an owl to recognize the man alongside you. Pistol Pete continued to blaze away at nothing in particular, apparently just raising hell for the fun of it—and you never could tell when one of his shells might score a lucky hit.

"With Bob's boat on one side, Stilly Taylor's on the other and the second yippie hauling at her nose, we strained and tugged at the grounded boat for more than an hour, trying to dislodge her, then threw overboard everything that wasn't screwed down and went through the whole procedure again, getting exactly nowhere.

"What time it was when radioman Purvis picked up a report that the Express was on the way, I'm not sure. When the hours are as long and tense as those were, you lose track of time. We were sweating and having the horrors, and every man was a bundle of nerves. The stricken boat hadn't budged.

"Now, with the Japs on the way down, we were in a fix. Even if they failed to spot us, which was unlikely, we'd be directly in their line of fire when they opened up on the island. It was time to get out of there, and fast. We had done all we could. With the tide running out, our chances of

LONG WERE THE NIGHTS

success were diminishing every minute. So we hauled in the tow-lines and prepared to depart.

"Maytag Charlie hastened our decision. You've heard of him, too, if you've read the papers. Like Pistol Pete he was an old friend of the Guadalcanal Marines, who had a number of other mellifluous names for him including 'Louie the Louse' and 'Washing-machine Charlie.'

"Charlie was a Nip pilot who flew an old crate that sounded like a riveting machine. You couldn't mistake him. Where he was based no one seemed to know, nor could anyone really figure out what his aim in life was. He was nocturnal and spent most of his time dropping flares.

"He must have seen us milling around down there, because suddenly a lovely white moon blossomed in the dark above us and came floating down. It was the biggest, brightest flare I'd ever seen, illuminating the night for yards around as it fell toward us. We were caught there like fish in a bowl. If Charlie had been toting a load of bombs, he could have blown us to kingdom come.

"We didn't linger after that. We had received orders by radio to abandon the grounded yippie and get the other one back to Tulagi safely. So with the Express now inside Savo Island and shelling Marine positions on Guadalcanal as it moved down through the channel, we lit for home."

"Lit" is hardly the word. The two PTs were responsible for the yippie and had to hold their speed down to his. They could not desert him to go after the enemy. Their mission

LONG WERE THE NIGHTS

was to get him back undetected.

For the thunder-boat men it was torture. Machinist's mate Nelson, from whom no engine could long hold a secret, threatened to climb aboard the yippie and "give her a shot in the pants." Radioman Cavanah, a little lad from Brooklyn with a fearsome voice, crouched on the forward deck and sang out the position of the approaching destroyers, which he could estimate by the flashes from their guns. "They're coming on down . . . two, three, four of them. We'll never make it on God's earth! Look at 'em come! We'll meet 'em head on! Boy, if we could only go *get* 'em!" Cavanah would have made a first-class train announcer.

The yippie did her best. By straining every seam, she made twelve knots, a performance which for her was unbelievable. She'd never done it before and probably never would again. But whether she and the escorting PTs would get across in front of the Japs, or run smack up against them, was in the hour-glass of the gods.

The mosquito boats' luck held. They made it.

"That trip," says Monty, "took two hours instead of the thirty minutes to which we in the PT boats were accustomed. For every soul aboard, those were the longest hours ever laid end to end. That unhappy damsel in the old comic song—the one who was bound hand and foot to the railroad tracks while the train roared down on her—would have known just how we felt.

"The Japs turned out to be a light force of destroyers and were jittery themselves, probably expecting to be set upon by another 'nineteen' torpedo boats. After a brief shelling of the island, they retired.

"But the thing I remember best is the half fifth of Scotch that Bob Wark produced from his locker when we were safely back at base.

" 'I've been saving this,' Bob said, 'for a very special occasion. What I had in mind was blowing up a battle-wagon or something stupendous. But hell, this is stupendous, too. Just imagine that yippie making twelve knots!'

" 'Just imagine,' I said.

"So at three o'clock in the morning we had a short one to the yippie, and felt a lot better. I never hope to taste finer Scotch."

Chapter Four

THE *McFarland* was hit that day. She was an old four-piper, built to combat German submarines in the other world war. When the Marines landed on Guadalcanal in August, she was there. Lately she had been carrying supplies up from the depots in the south.

This day, laden with gasoline and bombs and ammunition, she arrived off Lunga Point in the afternoon. All was quiet. Too quiet. Because the quiet days in that region of violence were the dangerous days, when the Japs put their heads together to plan new surprises.

The grounded yippie was still there on the reef. All efforts to dislodge her in the morning had been ineffectual, and a lucky hit from Pistol Pete had put a hole through her charthouse. Her crew had abandoned her and rowed ashore in their dinghy to await high tide again.

Despite the sporadic fire of Pistol Pete, who had once more ventured from his jungle hideout, the *McFarland* came in. Out from the beach sped Higgins boats to snatch the precious stuff she had brought and race ashore with it. The job of unloading got under way.

The afternoon waned. Over sea and island hills lay the deepening gray of dusk. Out of the sky came a flight of Jap dive-bombers.

The *Mac* was trapped. In that confined space, with Higgins boats alongside, there was not room for maneuvering. One by one the Japs peeled off, screamed down at her and loosed their loads. The little destroyer's guns fought back. She almost escaped. In the face of her withering fire the Jap Aichis dived frantically to their destruction, some of them exploding in mid air as the *Mac's* gunners found their targets. From Henderson Field sped a swarm of new, bright Lockheed Lightnings to give the embattled ship a hand.

But dusk had become darkness. Eluding the Lightnings, a lone Jap plunged from the murk and hurled himself at the destroyer in a last desperate assault. He hit her.

He was lucky. But for the depth charges racked on her stern, his bomb might have inflicted only a minor wound. Instead it exploded amid hundreds of pounds of TNT—and the TNT exploded with it. The *McFarland's* stern became suddenly a convulsive, writhing mass of metal.

Aboard her were Guadalcanal Marines en route from the island's hell to less violent regions for a well earned rest. Aboard, too, were some Marine wounded. Many were killed in the blast.

Miraculously the *Mac* remained afloat. She could even crawl a little, crookedly, like a dog with broken hind legs. But her stern was blown off, her rudder gone; her decks ran red with blood and her sick bay was jammed with wounded. She had to have help.

At PT headquarters on Tulagi, word came by radio that the *Mac* would attempt to reach that island but would need a pilot. Bob Wark volunteered. His boat, a pilot aboard, cleared harbor and raced to the *Mac's* assistance.

It was late then. The grounded yippie was at last afloat and had taken the crippled ship in tow. The PT, having delivered her pilot, stood by.

Then at Tulagi began the long, grim, gruesome task of moving the *McFarland's* dead and wounded. They were many, and the explosion of the depth charges had so mangled the ship's stern that her plates had to be cut away before some of the dead could be reached.

Officers and men of Squadron "X" labored through the night alongside those of the destroyer's crew who were able still to work. At dawn, weary and silent, they crept to the storehouse and lay down to sleep beside dead men wrapped in sheets.

If they had not known it before, they knew now they were fighting a war.

But in the days and nights that followed, the war they encountered was principally a war of nerves. The second four boats of the squadron had been delayed and were still en route. The tender had yet to arrive. With but three boats in service and no hope of repairing the fourth until equipment arrived, patrol duties were arduous.

All day, every day, the men worked on the boats. Guns had to be cleaned, repaired, adjusted. Torpedoes had to be readied. Engines had to be overhauled.

The boats had seen long hours of service and were temperamental. Like aging humans with too much work to do, they were often cranky. You didn't bully them. You coaxed

LONG WERE THE NIGHTS

them, teased them, flattered them into giving their best.

Jack Searles' boat, her bottom broken on the Florida Island reef, became of necessity a spare-part kit with which the others were kept in commission. Everything from spark plugs to fuel lines was stripped from her. Day by day she grew more naked, while her disconsolate crew prayed for the coming of the tender.

The tender? She was "somewhere on the way." But the Japs were methodically scouring the sea-lanes to Guadalcanal and bombing incoming ships wherever they could locate them. It was no simple task to find a way through their vigilance.

On Tulagi, as on Guadalcanal, sickness was common. The bite of a single mosquito could bring malaria, and there were swarms of mosquitoes. Dengue fever and dysentery ran rife, finding easy victims among men who, after working themselves into a state of exhaustion during the day, had to go out on patrol most of the night.

Stevenson, a radioman, was ill. Joe Nemec stumbled to his bed and stayed there. One after another the men were stricken, lost weight, became feverish, and had to quit.

"We were so full of quinine," Monty reports, "that the stuff was practically running out of our ears. It was hard to take, too. Having no capsules, we had to swallow the powder straight. You'd put the awful stuff into your mouth, gulp a glass of water to wash it down, and then go around choking and gagging for the next half hour. Nothing ever tasted quite so vile and bitter as that quinine powder.

"And to make matters worse, it kept coming back up—probably because we had so many things wrong with us. The taste lingered for hours, sometimes for a whole day, and then when you'd get over it and begin to feel vaguely like a human being again, it would be time to take some more."

Hardest hit of all, perhaps, was Squadron Commander Montgomery himself. He had not been well since that day in Panama when "Panama Flu" nearly canceled his trip to the fighting zone. At the first South Seas base, only half recovered from pneumonia, he had left his bed too soon. There had been no convalescence.

Now, terribly weak and sick, he went about in a fog of pain. The slightest exertion left him soaked with perspiration and struggling for breath. Slightly built to begin with, he was now twenty-five pounds lighter than normal and fast losing what little was left.

But the squadron did its job. By day the boats were kept in shape. At night they were taken out of hiding and sent into action—not always fully manned, and almost never with their original crews, but ready for whatever the Japs might send.

"Boats and crews," Montgomery recalls, "were all mixed up. One night we'd have Bob Searles at the helm of Stilly Taylor's boat, with some of Wark's crew. Another night Wark would take Bob's boat with some of Jack's crew. It didn't matter. The big thing was to get out there. Because

LONG WERE THE NIGHTS

the Japs were determined to land supplies for their troops on Guadalcanal, and our job was to prevent their doing it."

The base force personnel pitched in and helped. They were trained men, all of them. Many had worked with the boats before. Now they rode the boats almost as frequently as did the crews themselves.

"What really saved us from complete disintegration in those trying days," Bob Searles says, "was the moon. Happily it was beginning to brighten. The Japs were reluctant to come in without the protection of darkness. Our pilots on Henderson Field could make things too hot for them."

Moonlight to the men of Squadron "X" was not a reminder of romance and love lyrics. It was a heaven-sent reprieve. Afternoons they looked often and anxiously at the weather, cursing the sight of clouds, praying for a clear, bright night. But moon or no moon, the little PT boats slipped out of Tulagi at dusk to patrol the danger zone.

For recreation, when there was time for it, the men swam in the island's clear-water creeks or climbed to the lookout post behind their base to watch American airmen engage the Japs in dog-fights. They wrote letters to wives and sweethearts and mothers, and wondered if anyone would ever read them. They rode one another, talked of home, played poker. Mostly they played poker.

The stakes were often high. Money on Tulagi was worthless. Sometimes when a man was broke he played with Jap paper money captured by the Marines. Clean and crisp, printed by the Japs for use in Australia and the Dutch East Indies, it was plentiful and could be used for chips.

So went the days. Lorran Beed, when not sweating over engines, talked quietly about his family in Brooklyn. Old-timer Eldon Edwards, who had raked the bridge of a Jap destroyer with machine-gun fire the night of October 13, spun fabulous yarns of his adventures at sea. Charlie Tufts, the soul of the base force, tried to figure out some way to mount a torpedo tube on one of the tiny landing-boats so that he, personally, could go Jap hunting—and but for lack of time he might have succeeded.

Bracy built his famous lemon pies. Peterson and Barnard, machinist's mates, thought up new pranks to play on each other. Wisdom beefed. Big Bill Nelson doped the engines and chuckled when they pleased him. Ship's cook Carl Todd of the same crew practised diligently with a forty-five and could hit a parrot on the wing.

The moon rode high.

Then the moon shriveled. The nights grew dark again. Every hour of patrol duty was another rasping stroke of the file against nerves already rubbed ragged.

"We kept seeing things on those patrols," says Bob. "At that time our radios were not yet on aircraft frequency, and we could never be sure what was going on. Often the reconnaissance reports from Guadalcanal would fail to reach us on time. Then we'd have to go out blind, not knowing what to expect.

"When that happened, we were hypersensitive to every

little thing. The outline of a palm tree on shore, its branches waving in the wind, would look like an approaching plane. Starlight on the sea became the wake of an enemy ship. Our hearing became abnormally acute and every smallest sound made us jump.

"You'll never know how long a night can be until you've been through that sort of thing."

There were some lighter moments, however. One day machinist's mate Ray Long got up from a game of red-dog and went for a stroll in the jungle. When he returned, he was tenderly transporting a small round ball of fur that made sounds like a sewing-machine.

"How would a kitten get to a God-forsaken place like this?" he wanted to know.

No one could supply an answer. But the creature in Long's arms was undeniably a kitten. Not a Solomon Islands kitten either—if there are such things—but a common, back-porch variety of American house cat, small, very cute, and altogether black.

The boys took it to their squadron commander, whose wife, Mary, is fond of cats. They pondered a name for it. Said ship's cook Steve Mehes: "We ought to call the rascal 'Tulagi,' account of he's black as a Tulagi night."

"Tulagi" was ceremoniously christened.

Said machinist's mate Cline: "Most likely he's a Marine cat. That's bad. He ought to be in the navy."

Chief yeoman George Hausen was called in. He was a

happy man. His rich baritone voice could be heard at all hours, frightening the parrots with a song he had either heard somewhere or made up for his own amusement. "Oh She Flew Through The Air Like A Goose" was the name of it. Was it legally possible, the men wished to know, to enlist "Tulagi" in the United States Navy?

Said Hausen solemnly: "In this tropical paradise, anything is possible."

Shipping papers were forthwith made out, and with full and solemn ceremony the new arrival was inducted. He had the run of the base, slept with the men, and became the squadron's pet.

Mary Montgomery would have loved it.

On the twenty-second day of October the tender came. She had had her share of troubles. Enemy planes had attacked her, and there had been a brush with a Jap submarine, but somehow she had managed to get through unscathed.

She was a lovely sight. The men stood and cheered as she dropped anchor in Tulagi's little harbor. They shook the hand of her skipper, Lieutenant Commander Beasley, and called him fond names.

With the tender came the rest of the base force personnel, and now there was some relief for men who had worked night and day without rest to keep things running. Below decks were food and medical supplies. The future looked brighter.

LONG WERE THE NIGHTS

"We moved the tender to a jungle stream near by," Montgomery says, "and went to work at once to camouflage her. The stream was not very wide. Some of the men shinnied up the palm trees on the banks and extended the foliage right over the ship. Then we hacked off a lot of branches and palm leaves and decorated her from bow to stern, to keep the Japs at a distance.

"It was an artistic job. When we were finished, she looked just like a beer garden. All she lacked was a troupe of singing waiters and an orchestra. And, of course, the beer.

"But if we were glad to see the tender, we were just about delirious two days later when the second four boats of the squadron arrived. Even the Marines on Guadalcanal must have heard us celebrating that night!"

Chapter Five

THE four motor torpedo boats which arrived at Tulagi October 24 at once took up their share of the burden, participating in patrols that very night.

One was captained by Lieutenant Hugh Robinson, the squadron executive officer, called "Robbie" by his fellows. He hails from Springfield, Mass. Another was in charge of Lieutenant Lester H. Gamble of San Francisco, who was to become the squadron's high scorer, and who, with his crew, perfected a technique which gave the Japs a perpetual headache.

Another new boat was skippered by Lieutenant (jg) James Brent Greene, a southern young man from Frankfort, Kentucky, with an acute aversion to spiders—about which more later. The fourth was Leonard Nikoloric's boat.

For their first major action, the officers and men of these four boats had to wait until October 29. They were then soundly and violently initiated.

The Japs were in deadly earnest that night. Tired of being harassed and chased by a few (nineteen?) persistent mosquito boats, they put together a striking force of nine or ten destroyers and descended through the slot to resume their nocturnal shelling of Guadalcanal. Patrol planes spotted them and the word went out.

Gathered about the radio in the PT squadron office, the

LONG WERE THE NIGHTS

men received the news with assorted emotions. To the now veteran boat captains who had been on the job since October 12, the tidings were grim. They no longer bragged lightly of the battle-wagons they would sink. They had learned the hard way that enemy ships were not easily sunk, and that a stalked victim more often than not had sharp claws when brought to bay.

But to the officers and men of the newly arrived contingent, the call to action was a tocsin. They were impatient. Their trip to the fighting zone had been long and tedious.

Quartermaster Lee Bagby ached for an opportunity to try out his really remarkable knowledge of navigation. Gunner's mate Roy Beckers, in love with his guns, longed to see a Jap in his sights. Typical of all was machinist's mate John Der, of Nikoloric's boat, who stroked the wings of an enormous, full-blown eagle tattooed on his chunky chest and said, "Aw, the hell with 'em! We'll sink 'em all!"

Six of the PTs slipped out of Tulagi that night to meet the enemy. The boat skippered by Brent Greene stole past Savo Island and lay waiting in the slot to spot the approaching ships and trail them down. The Searles brothers and Stilly Taylor were also out spotting. Robinson, Kendall and Nikoloric lay waiting in ambush. Boldly the Japs came in. But as so often happened, the carefully formed plans of the PT skippers were jogged by events unforeseen.

"We were uneasily waiting for the 'Japes' to show up," Bob says, "and also had an ear cocked for some word from Brent Greene, who was farther up the line. We

LONG WERE THE NIGHTS

got the word, all right. Brent had sighted the incoming ships and was trailing them. But he lost them in the dark. It was very dark. It was nearly always very dark out there in Sleepless Lagoon when the Japs attacked Guadalcanal.

"Suddenly, while waiting for further word from Greene, we were snapped to attention by the growl of an airplane above us, and in the sky almost directly overhead a brilliant flare broke out. Dead ahead was a Jap destroyer.

"The plane was one of ours—either a Marine patrol plane or one of the navy scouts which had been doing yeoman work trying to keep us posted on what the Japs were up to. He may have seen us and dropped the flare to warn us. More likely, having spotted some movement on the sea below, he'd been trying to find out what was going on. We never did see him clearly—just a swift, dark shape in the sky, a roar in the night, and then he was gone. But that big, bright moon of a flare was slowly falling toward us, turning night to day.

"On the destroyer the Japs must have been scared, not knowing how many planes were up there or what might hit them. Ignoring us, they cut loose with their anti-aircraft guns, and we were deafened by the pulsing *whuffs* of their defensive barrage.

"But they didn't keep at it long. Before we had time to try for a shot, the Jap lowered his guns and bore down on us, wide open. His AAs gave us a merciless raking, and it was one of those hairlifting moments when anything can happen."

LONG WERE THE NIGHTS

Almost everything did happen. At such close range, with only the knife-edge bow of the onrushing destroyer at which to aim, the PT boat was in no position to fire her torpedoes. Torpedoes are not rifle bullets; they must have a target of respectable dimensions. The Jap could have fishtailed, one side or the other, to dodge anything that was sent at him. He knew it, and the sea curled white at his bow as he rushed in for the kill.

The PT turned and ran. With all three engines blending in a single thunder-throated roar, she sped through the enemy's curtain of fire and made for the western end of Tulagi, hoping to lead the Jap past the striking force led by Robbie.

But she suddenly didn't have the speed.

"It was just one of those things," says Bob. "Ordinarily there isn't a Jap afloat who can match the speed of our Packard 4Ms, and until then our engines had bent over backward to be good to us—done all we ever asked of them and more than they were ever designed to do, both in speed and hours of operation. But they were fouled now from the grind of slow-speed patrolling, and our top speed was suddenly not the forty-five to fifty knots we needed, but a dismal twenty. The Jap could do better than that without straining a seam."

The destroyer was gaining. Its AA guns sang a louder, swifter song, and the bristling 4.7s belched flame from its forward turrets. The PT groaned on through spouting geysers of ocean, raked by shellfire in which it seemed only a miracle could keep her unscathed. All about her the night was blotchily bright with explosions.

"Make smoke!" Bob ordered.

Scottie Lueckert pawed at the generator. The heavenly white cloud poured out astern.

"Tell Robbie what's up! Tell him we're coming!"

Paul Stephenson shivered at the radio. He was a big man, brave as the best, but for days had been fighting off fever. Nevertheless his voice went derisively, steadily out through the thunder of the guns and the labored thudding of the boat's engines.

"William is chasing us!" he chanted. "William is chasing us! Hurry, hurry!" "William" was the PT code word for Jap.

"When the striking force picked up that yell," says Nick, "we already knew that Bob and Jack were in trouble. We knew the Apes were in there somewhere and we were chasing up and down in the dark, trying to find something to shoot at. Suddenly we saw the flares from the plane and of course heard the gunfire. We could see the smoke and enemy shells dropping like rain into the white billows."

Nick remembers that night too well. It was his first action. He and his men had gone out with the eagerness of kids at a carnival, sure of themselves and their boat. Not all were as noisily belligerent as John Der, with his "Aw, the hell with 'em, we'll sink 'em all!"—but they were taut and ready.

Now the Searles brothers were in terrible danger. It was not a carnival. It was all at once fearfully personal.

LONG WERE THE NIGHTS

Bob, Jack and Nick were friends. They had been together at Princeton. They had gone to football games and dances together; knew the same girls; had gone navy together.

Nick began to sweat. He knew that if anything happened to Bob and Jack Searles, it would be Nikoloric who walked up Woodridge Place in Leonia, New Jersey, and climbed the steps of number 123, and rang the bell. "You'll be the one standing there," he thought, "when Mrs. Searles opens that door. You'll be the one to tell her . . ."

"I was scared stiff," Nick confesses humbly.

The three boats in the striking force moved swiftly to cut off the pursuing destroyer. Robbie and Kendall went to the right. Nick shoved the throttles up and sent the boat roaring to the left, into the smoke.

His boat responded beautifully. She had not yet been fouled by an overdose of patrolling and her honey-smooth engines were the pride and joy of machinist's mate Alsie Porterfield, who tinkered with them day and night. She drilled a tunnel through the choking cloud of smoke and left a hissing spray-snake in her wake.

That she might have encountered a major part of the enemy fleet on the other side of the smoke was, of course, at least a possibility. This being a night of surprises, anything might happen.

She did not roar into any Jap fleet. Or into the destroyer, either. The smoke was thick, the darkness thicker. The PT emerged at top speed into nothingness, just in time to see the explosion as Brent Greene and his crew made the kill.

LONG WERE THE NIGHTS

Greene, off the western end of Guadalcanal, had also heard the radioed call for help. Beside him in the cockpit stood quartermaster Lee Bagby, who was acting exec that night. Anxiously they searched the darkness for a sign of the Jap and her quarry. Over at ten o'clock someone was catching hell.

Said Bagby a few seconds later: "That's it, skipper. Ten o'clock. That's it, all right." His voice was low and he was very calm.

Greene fingered the throttles and turned the boat gently into position. They could see the destroyer plainly. For a moment his guns had been silent, but his turrets were now spouting flames again. Ahead of him, weaving and dodging in desperation, was the unhappy PT.

Suddenly the Jap turned away, still firing as he abandoned the chase. He may have sensed trouble. He may have known that the PT striking force was closing in for combat. In any case he turned—and swung directly into Greene's sights.

Torpedoman Goddard stood ready at the tubes, mallet upraised to fire by percussion if the impulse failed to function. Stayonovitch and Ratcliff manned the fifties, jaws jutting as they awaited the word. With engines turning barely enough to keep her steady, and making no sound audible to the enemy above the thunder of his own big guns, the PT stealthily closed.

The Jap saw his peril and opened fire.

"Now!" Bagby breathed.

Brent Greene nodded. The torpedoes sped from their

LONG WERE THE NIGHTS

tubes, splashed into the sea and ran. Every man on the boat held his breath.

The Jap was hurling everything he had at the plywood sliver when he blew up. The thunder of his guns was smothered by a louder roar, and a sheet of flame leaped skyward from his stern. He shuddered from the sea as though tossed by a giant wave, hung crazily in space for a second, then dropped. His whole stern was furiously ablaze.

So great was the concussion that the men on the PT were rocked. They recovered quickly. The Jap did not. Mortally wounded, he fled through the night toward home, trailing his blazing tail.

He never got there. Air scouts found him at dawn, gutted and sinking.

There was no more action that night. The rest of the enemy fleet did not linger but turned back, its mission abandoned. The Japs were fast learning that the hitherto uncontested waters between Guadalcanal and Tulagi were no longer safe for them.

And the PT men had learned something, too, from that night's sortie, but theirs was a lesson learned the pleasant way in the satisfaction of a job well done. They had demonstrated dramatically the value of teamwork and cooperation. One such demonstration was worth a hundred classroom lectures, and was to serve them well in later engagements.

For his coolness and competence in action, quartermaster

LONG WERE THE NIGHTS

Lee Bagby won the Silver Star. And another Jap flag was painted on the PT emblem at Sesapi.

The Japs stayed at home the next few nights, and with seven boats in commission it was now possible to assign the nightly patrols in such a way that most of the men were given every other night off. Jack Searles' boat, snagged on the Florida reef, was undergoing repairs in the shop established by carpenter's mates Wallace and Swede Olsen.

The men needed the rest. Japs or no Japs, the patrols were hard on human endurance. Complete relaxation, reprieve from duty, was the only cure. Unfortunately there could be no reprieve from the heat, the rain, the mosquitoes.

Joe Nemec, "Silent Joe," who was gentle, quiet and liked by everyone, succumbed to peritonitis. Paul Stephenson, feverish for days, at last was sent out to recover. Bob Wark was ill and left, too, and his boat was placed in command of Tom Kendall. Air raid alarms were frequent. The Jap navy nursed its sores at Bougainville.

At every opportunity, pharmicist's mate Donald Lee Perkins dug foxholes. Foxholes were Doc's hobby. One day he was digging another of them when electrician's mate "Frenchy" Dufresne came suddenly on the scene.

Said Frenchy: "You're wasting your time. Did the Apes ever bomb this place?"

"Some day they will," said Doc. "Some Sunday. Ever since Pearl Harbor, the Japs think every American goes to

LONG WERE THE NIGHTS

church on Sunday, or sleeps. Furthermore," continued Doc, "the fact that they haven't yet bombed Tulagi is no indication they won't. Over on Guad, the Marines have foxholes everywhere."

Industriously he plied his shovel. When the enemy did bomb Tulagi, he meant to be ready.

"You're wasting your time," said Frenchy again.

"The Japs like us, you think?"

"It isn't a question of liking us. Look, now. Bombs cost money. It costs money to lug 'em. Bougainville is quite a hike from here." Frenchy put his legs apart at the edge of the hole and gravely studied the digger. "You think after they lug those bombs all the way down here from Bougainville, they'd be dumb enough to waste 'em on Tulagi? What they're after is Henderson Field!"

"Perhaps," said Perkins. Methodically he went on digging.

"They get Henderson Field," argued Dufresne, "and our goose is really cooked. Anybody knows that. The day those monkeys set a plane down on Henderson, we're through. We'll be lucky to get out the back door before they take this island over."

As a matter of fact, the enemy did land a plane on Henderson Field. He landed several. So certain was he that one of his combined air and sea offensives would meet with success that at dawn one day, after a bloody night of battle, a squadron of Zeros serenely swept in to make a landing.

But the enemy's transports and escorting warships had

been sent to the bottom. His troops on the island had died by the hundreds in fanatic but futile attempts to storm Marine positions, and were piled high against the wire. Marine pilots gave the incoming Zeros a blistering reception.

On Tulagi, however, Doc Perkins dug his foxholes all over the place, while his mates stood by to offer suggestions more ribald then helpful.

"Some Sunday," Doc insisted, "we'll get it. Anyway, this is first rate exercise."

The patrols continued. On the night of November 6, Stilly Taylor encountered three enemy destroyers near Savo Island, fired a torpedo at one of them and may have hit it. The Japs gave chase and held him in a withering cross-fire. Stilly eluded them.

The following night Les Gamble scored the first of his impressive string of victories.

Lieutenant Lester Gamble was a young man of many accomplishments. Good-looking, popular with the girls, he had worked once in a San Francisco night club and from contact with all kinds of people had acquired both a sense of humor and a broad philosophy.

He was cool and contained, hard to excite, and had the soul of a gambler. Time and again he proved his well-developed knack of knowing the enemy's mind.

"We were on patrol that night at the western end of Lengo Channel," Nick says, "covering the coast between Koli Point and Taivu, where the Japs had been putting ashore some troops. Three of us were out, all concentrating in that sector. It was a gusty, fairly dark night, the sea too rough for comfort. Sure enough, the enemy came in.

"As it happened, however, he came in later than usual and we had begun to think we were due for a night of peace and quiet. Ten to two were usually the fertile hours. If nothing happened by two, you could begin to hope nothing would, and on our boat that was usually the time for Charlie May, the cook, to emerge from the galley with coffee and sandwiches.

"It was about one o'clock when we sighted the enemy. John Legg, the quartermaster, was on watch, standing beside the starboard gun turret, searching the sea through glasses. He was tireless, that man. His knowledge of navigation was remarkable, and he liked nothing better than to put his talents to use. Matter of fact, Legg did most of our navigating all the time we were out there in the Solomons. He never made a mistake.

"All at once he lowered the glasses and turned to the bridge, where I was standing with Bernie O'Neill, the boat's exec.

" 'The Japs,' Legg said, 'are with us.' He didn't raise his voice. He almost never raised his voice. He was as quiet, as well mannered, as efficient as any man in the squadron."

Nick snatched the glasses and had a look. What he saw was an enemy destroyer, unaware of danger and moving west toward Koli Point.

The PT moved in. There was all the time in the world to

get set for a shot. The Jap was entirely unaware of what lay in store for him.

Legg took the glasses again and his quiet voice tolled off the enemy's progress. Porterfield talked to his engines below. Owen Pearle stood by the radio. Marvin Crosson checked the tubes. "Twenty knots," Legg said. "He's doing twenty. About twenty, sir. We're off a hair. Off left. That's better. Steady on course now . . . steady . . . just a shade closer, sir . . ."

The Jap's speed and position made him a perfect target.

"Now, sir," said Legg.

All four torpedoes went singing. The crew held its collective breath for the interminable few seconds that would indicate success or failure.

There was no explosion. The torpedoes had missed.

Said machinist's mate Charlie Carner, an old hand who'd been around long enough to accept failure philosophically: "What the hell, skipper, there'll be others. Don't look so glum." Then over the radio came the voice of Robbie's radioman, Hamilton. Robbie had seen enough to know something was up. Hamilton begged frantically for information.

"Poor old Robbie," says Nick. "He never did get a look at that Jap because he was farthest away and practically out of it. He kept screaming for 'the dope' and neither Les nor I had time to give him any. He just about went out of his mind."

LONG WERE THE NIGHTS

Les Gamble had seen the Jap, too. Moving cozily through the dark, he had put himself in position to intercept the enemy off the bulge of Koli Point. When the Jap saw the wakes of the torpedoes which had missed him, he quickly changed course. Les outguessed him and shifted first.

That was the Gamble technique: don't hurry, just sit and wait. Conditions had to be just right before the method could be put into practice, of course, but Gamble more often than not created the conditions by anticipating the enemy's movements. His crew said he was psychic.

This time the enemy never knew what hit him. A spread of four torpedoes hissed at him from out of nowhere, and at least one, probably more, perhaps all of them, exploded with a roar in the destroyer's vitals.

Out over the air to Nikoloric and Hugh Robinson came the triumphant voice of the radioman, Eldon Alvis, elatedly singing: "We got a hit! We got a hit! We're heading for the barn!"

Score one for Gamble and Company—the first of many.

Chapter Six

"You guys may like the idea of squatting around on cots for the next couple of years," said Wisdom, emptying his dungaree pockets of nails which he had pilfered from the carpenter shop, "but me, I got to have comforts."

Snorting disdainfully, he sawed a board in half and nailed the pieces into place. Under his capable hands a sturdy chair was taking shape.

The men grinned. But Wisdom worked on. In front of his tent lay an assortment of lumber and tools, also borrowed from the shop. Wiz was busy building furniture. It was very good furniture, too.

"The trouble with you guys," he growled, "you're not civilized."

"Maybe," said Teddy Kuharski, "you figure to be here forever, huh? Maybe you expect to settle down and raise a family here."

Wisdom's hammer banged away without interruption. He put the chair beside a table he had constructed, then hauled another slab of lumber from the pile and applied try-square and pencil. Something puzzled him. Scratching his chin, he sat in the newly finished chair and for a moment was deep in thought.

Some of the others were building furniture, too—inspired, perhaps, by Wisdom's energy and the undeniable need for a few crude comforts. This particular group had moved into a section of Sesapi located midway between the huddled shacks on the shore and the lookout post on the bluff. They referred to it as "Snob Hill" and considered it an exclusive suburb.

George Gilpin came up. He was Brent Greene's radioman, a dark-haired southern lad with a sly sense of humor and a grin that could be hidden when necessary behind a studied lack of expression. "I got an idea," he said. "We ought to have some street signs around here to keep you guys from getting lost."

"We ought to have some streets, too," said O'Malley, "to get lost on."

"Will you birds shut up?" groused Wisdom. "I'm concentrating."

"He's concentrating," said Roy Beckers. "Everybody stand back."

"We need a place to shoot the breeze," Wisdom said. "We need a bench. I'm going to build a bench."

"The Seat of Meditation," said O'Malley.

"He don't mean that kind of bench," Gilpin argued. "Besides, where would we get any mail-order catalogs in this place?"

"I mean a bench to sit on," said Wisdom. "So we can enjoy the view here and shoot the breeze. It gets too damn' hot inside these tents and shacks, and there's too many bugs. Leave me alone, you guys. I got to dope out a bench."

He built one. It was finished a couple of days later and

occupied a place of honor on "Main Street," where the boys could sit and look out over the settlement below and the sea beyond. On clear days the sea was a soft, translucent green, very pretty.

Inspired by Wisdom's work, the occupants of Snob Hill shed their dungarees in the broiling heat of those long afternoons and pitched in to make their surroundings homelike. They swept out the native huts and constructed shelves and cupboards. They put up pictures of wives and sweethearts, built tables for red-dog and poker, dug trenches to carry off the rain water which otherwise would have inundated them.

It was very hot. Though nearly naked, the men oozed perspiration which attracted swarms of insects. Behind them Tulagi's gaudy hills rose tawny and green, flecked with flowers and streaked by the passage of brilliant red and snowy white parrots. It was an unhealthy gaudiness, dank and stifling. No one was eager to explore it.

Tables and chairs grew in abundance, and the "snobs" enjoyed unheard-of comforts in their high suburb. On the Seat of Meditation the problems of the war were solved in solemn bull-sessions.

Howard Peterson remembered the good times in Panama. Gunner's mate Leon Nale, a tall, slender lad from Alabama, talked wistfully of the girls he knew. Gilpin and O'Malley ribbed each other. John Legg taught other quartermasters the finer points of navigation. It was a little like a front porch at home.

LONG WERE THE NIGHTS

"These islands," said one of the men one evening; "these lousy, stinking islands—what good are they? For all of me the Japs can have 'em. Nobody but a goddam Jap would want 'em!"

Said Crosson gently: "They are not islands. Guadalcanal is not an island. They're points on a map."

"So all right. Let the Japs have 'em."

"That's just it. The Japs did have them, and it was important for us to win them back. Look here." Crosson took a dog-eared map from his pocket and spread it on his knees. "Here we are, right here. North of us the enemy is solid, with a string of stepping-stones all the way down from Japan. South are Australia and the sea-lanes we must use to defend it. From Guadalcanal the Japs could cover those sea-lanes with bombers. See?"

They had known it anyway. Grousing was merely an outlet for cramped emotions. But when the war was over and the Japs were liquidated, Guadalcanal and Tulagi could turn turtle and sink into the sea, for all these men cared. They wouldn't shed a tear.

A poker game was in progress one afternoon—ship's cook Frank O'Malley red hot as always—when the glittering sun was engulfed suddenly by swift clouds that let loose a flood. The men scurried for shelter. When it rained on Tulagi, you took no chances.

They plucked their personal possessions from the floors of huts and tents, hung them on anything handy, and pulled up their feet in the manner of a plane retracting its landing gear. Then dolefully they watched the ground about them turn into a sticky sea of mud. Without the drains they had constructed, Snob Hill would have been a complete washout. Tulagi weather was savage.

The Marines on Guadalcanal knew all about this freakish weather. They had been living and dying in it from the beginning, and their airmen had found it a foe almost as treacherous as the Jap. So did the overworked pilots of a handful of SOC biplanes based on Tulagi.

Brave men flew these navy planes. They were the eyes of the PT boats, tirelessly searching the seas for signs of enemy activity. The weather made little difference to them. They knew that bad weather was a favorite weapon of the Japs, and beneath or behind any advancing front of swollen clouds, enemy warships were likely to be on the prowl. Consequently they went out in the worst of it, under impossible conditions.

The day of the poker game, one of them did not come back.

At the base, work went steadily on. Stan Thomas, who could make a torpedo talk, was in charge of the torpedo shop, where he and Shorty Long and Herb Wing had little time to be concerned about Tulagi's weather. Sun or rain, they were everlastingly occupied with the boats. It was a six hour job to get a tin fish ready for firing, and the fish were fired often.

"Ten thousand bucks it costs," said Shorty, "to send one

of these babies on its way. We have to be sure they get what they're sent for."

Other men were transferred from boats to base whenever the squadron as a whole had need of their talents. Arthur Stuffert left to work in the engine shop. Charlie May was coaxed against his will to slave in the shore galley. Some of the men liked the change; some didn't. Most of them preferred the boats. Typical was ship's cook Lloyd Hummer, who ducked his chores ashore and rode a PT boat at every opportunity, praying for action.

"Just lemme at 'em," he begged. "We'll show those Apes!"

The man who really ran the base force was chief boatswain's mate Charlie Tufts. Nothing stumped Charlie. No job was too big or too pesky. When tools or parts were needed, he sometimes took a walk—usually to the Marine encampment.

One day, returning from such a stroll, Charlie ambled solemnly into the torpedo shop and began emptying his pockets. A wrench came out. A handful of nuts and bolts. A weird and varied assortment of odds and ends for which the PT men had been tearing their hair.

Charlie blinked at his collection. He was a mild man, a little bumpy in places, running short of hair but never of energy or ingenuity. "Now how in the world," he said, "did I ever get all this stuff? My, my! Someone must have framed me."

These were the lighter interludes. Some of the others

were less happily remembered. Like the night of November 7.

Robbie, Brent and Nick were patrolling that night within shouting distance of each other, and about midnight the Japs came in. Brent maneuvered for a shot and fired a spread of four torpedoes at the leading enemy ship, a destroyer.

One of the fish jammed in its tube. A fountain of sparks leaped skyward and the quiet night was bedlam. Torpedoman Goddard cleared the tube with a blow of his mallet.

The torpedoes may have winged home or may not. No one was sure. At any rate the Jap was still in action, and the dazzling fireworks of the hot run had given him a point of aim for his searchlights. In a heart-beat of time, Robbie and Brent were trapped in the lights while the Jap's big guns roared their defiance.

The enemy was on his toes that night, performing at peak efficiency. His shooting was good. Too good. A salvo of 4.7s screamed from his main battery, and one of them exploded with an earthquake roar on the bow of Robbie's boat.

Happily, every man on the mosquito boat was at his battle station. All were tossed about like tenpins, but none was forward when the shell struck, and none was seriously hurt. Where the bow of the boat had been, however, was now only a jagged mass of plywood splinters. The PT opened fire with her fifties and struggled to escape.

"We in our boat," says Nick, "heard the explosion just

after getting in a shot. We saw what happened. Robbie's boat was less than a hundred yards abeam of us, and the glare of the shell-burst lit up the night all around us.

"We thought it was all over for Robbie and his gang. If that shell hadn't finished them, the next hit certainly would. The Japs were sending everything they had at her."

Pearle, Nick's radioman, sent a yell over the radio to find out who was alive over there. Someone was, because the PT's machine-guns were crackling. But after what had happened there *had* to be casualties.

"Are you okay?" Pearle begged. "Are you all right?"

It was Robinson himself who answered. "Hell, yes!" he barked. "We're heading for home!"

Despite the loss of her bow, the crippled boat was running with all the speed she could manage, executing a series of wobbly maneuvers that kept the enemy's shells wide of the mark. Meanwhile gunner's mate Ben Parrish, wedged in his turret, clung fast to the grips of his guns and coolly shot out the destroyer's searchlights. It was very sweet shooting.

The boat churned on, throwing up fountains of spray. She was getting away. But the Japs had a perfect target. The smoke generator had jammed, and the Jap had the range.

Chief torpedoman Alfred Norwood, an old-timer with what was needed, started for the smoke pot. Soaking wet, half blinded, barely able to keep his feet on the twisting deck, he fell on the generator and tore at it with his hands.

It *had* to work. Without smoke, the boat was doomed.

There on his knees, Norwood wrestled with the valves while enemy shells cracked overhead like whips.

The valves let go and smoke gushed out—but backward.

Now the smoke used on the motor torpedo boats is a chemical mixture shot forth under pressure. It is thick and strangling. It burns cruelly, like acid, and can sear the skin off a man's face or hands very quickly.

Norwood was caught in the hissing stream and stumbled back out of it, his face and arms in torment. But he went back in. He got his hands on the balky generator and stayed there, pounding it, until the smoke poured out the way it was supposed to. In all this time the enemy's fire had not diminished.

With the white screen swelling in her wake, the PT at last shook off pursuit and left the Jap astern. Then Norwood looked at his hands.

They were bright red, covered with thin, bulging blisters that broke and peeled away. They were aflame to the elbows.

Norwood walked forward on the heaving deck and sat down by the port turret and was sick. But without question his coolness and ability in a grave emergency had saved the lives of his boatmates.

It was that way often on the little thunder boats. Fate put the finger on some one man and challenged him. "Brother, it's your turn." The chosen individual might be the skipper, the second in command, a man at the guns or a machinist's mate in the engine-room. Officers or enlisted men—it made no difference. Fate played no favorites.

Suddenly for a brief, bright flash of time, the lives of all aboard would depend on one man's ability and courage. None knew when his turn might come.

The PT made port that night, limping through the dark with the sea growling in her vitals. It was incredible, but it happened. The Jap who had crippled her was less lucky. Too avid for the kill, he forgot the other boat and left himself unprotected. His searchlight beams and the bright light of his gunbursts were a tempting target.

The other PT, with Nick at the wheel, Bernie O'Neill and John Legg spotting, had stalked him half way across the slot. Now she slipped up on his silent side, away from the thunder of his guns, and loosed her torpedoes.

A few hours later chief yeoman John Wicks stood on an upturned box in front of the squadron office and, with red and white paint dripping brightly from his brush, added yet another Jap flag to the PT emblem. The Marines on Guadalcanal could sleep a little easier.

But November brought a note of sadness. Lieutenant Commander Alan Montgomery, the squadron's skipper, had reached the end of his rope. Worn out at last by the after-effects of his "Panama Flu," which had not been influenza at all, the commander was gravely ill and was ordered home to get well. For weeks he had been living on fortitude and sulfa drugs. Now not even these were sufficient to keep him on his feet.

The officers and men of Squadron "X" were glum. They liked their skipper. He had been one of the fairest, most understanding men they had ever known, and had seemed to know just what to say and do when they had the blues or the jitters. In Panama he had put them through some training paces which at times had seemed grueling, but even then he had given more of himself than he asked of his men.

"Moreover," Nick says, "the commander was a wonderfully human guy, always, and had a rare sense of humor. Some of us who'd been to Eastern colleges used to kid him sometimes about being an Annapolis man. 'Let's see now,' we'd say. 'The commander went to some trade school somewhere, didn't he? What *was* the name of that place?' He'd grin and kid us right back about being a bunch of mere boys from the Ivy League. I don't know whether this kind of comradeship runs through the whole navy or is restricted to the PT unit where *esprit de corps* is naturally tremendous, but I do know we felt like hell when the skipper had to leave us. It was one of the darkest hours of the whole campaign."

It was a dark hour for Monty, too. "As I've mentioned before," he explains, "we were not a sentimental bunch. At least, I don't think we were, and I'm sure we seldom showed it if we were. Most of the camaraderie Nick mentions came out in clowning or heated bull sessions, or in long hours of talk about tactics and so on. But I'd never known a finer gang of boys than these, and it hurt terribly to have to leave them at a time when they were facing danger and death night after night with a chance of being killed.

"A PT boat is not a battleship. You get to know the moods and thoughts of every man who works with you. Even when you put eight of those little boats together, forming a squadron, you still have only a relatively small group of men and the feeling of closeness is retained. I was more than physically sick when I had to say good-by."

But Montgomery had to go. One morning in early November, having turned his command over to Lieutenant Hugh Robinson, squadron executive officer and skipper, Monty climbed into a plane. He had to be helped into it.

The men shook his hand and wished him Godspeed. The plane took off, bound for New Caledonia, on the first leg of the commander's homeward journey. The men watched the speck in the sky until it disappeared.

"Many of us," Bob Searles recalls, "wondered if we would ever see him again, and we all thought bitterly what a rotten war this was—what a lousy, rotten war it was, after all."

Chapter Seven

"On our nights off," says Bob, "we sometimes went to the movies. Don't look amazed. We really did.

"Lieutenant Commander Beasley had a moving-picture projector in the crew's mess hall on the tender. It wasn't exactly Radio City, but we were able to crowd a fair-sized audience in there and the shows were a wonderful antidote for patrol tension.

"The commander had about half a dozen old films including *The Great Dictator* with Charlie Chaplin, which is the one we remember best, and sometimes we were lucky enough to obtain other pictures from ships coming in with supplies.

"We used to rotate them. After the boys had seen the entire repertoire, they'd begin at the beginning and go through it all over again.

"It was quite an achievement to sit through one of those pictures. The commander was inconsiderate as hell—no plush seats, no air conditioning; just a few hard chairs and Charlie Chaplin or Rita Hayworth or whoever happened to be on the program that night. And I want to tell you it was hot.

"We'd sit there, the men stripped to their skivvies and the officers with their shirts thrown open, all of us sweating like patrons of a Finnish bath and enduring the torments of the damned, just for the privilege of watching a few stale movies which most of us had seen back in the States.

"We laughed uproariously at the antics of Charlie Chaplin, and heaved heavy sighs at sight of the beautiful gals who were so cool and luscious and never did any sweating. The boys made wise-cracks and had themselves a time.

"Some of us saw *The Great Dictator* at least a dozen times, and got to know it so well we could have donned Charlie's costumes and done the whole routine ourselves. Toward the end, the men were trying hard to figure out some way to run the films backward, just for variety."

Most of the time, however, the men provided their own amusement. One had a guitar, and when the Tulagi moon was full and bright and the Japs stayed at home, the men gathered around to listen to the music.

The songs varied. Hausen could always conjure up smiles with "She Flew Through The Air Like A Goose." Beckers, Ed Edwards and the other old-timers were never tongue-tied.

The most popular songs, however, were the sentimental ones. Hawaiian ballads. The girl back home. The little white house in the valley.

The *McFarland*, towed into Tulagi October 16, had been moved to a creek-mouth a few miles distant, and occasionally the PT men paid her a visit. An epic of human fortitude and ingenuity was being enacted on the *Mac*.

Day after day under a ceiling of camouflage which made

the heat almost unendurable, the sweating members of her crew swarmed over her, rebuilding her blown-off stern. They had few tools other than their hands. The timbers they needed had to be hacked out of the jungle. Jap steel was hauled from an abandoned enemy submarine base on a nearby island.

They were determined to get her out of there and were slaving night and day to do it. Already a grotesque but workable jury rudder was beginning to take shape.

"We used to go over there," Nick says, "for the luxury of a hot shower, and when we returned and told the boys at the base what was going on at McFarland Creek, some of them wouldn't believe it. You couldn't do a job like that without proper tools and equipment, they insisted. They had to go down and see for themselves."

Air-raid alarms were a daily occurrence at that time. The Japs were hitting Guadalcanal hard, trying to soften the island for an all-out attempt to recapture it before our Marines could be reinforced. When the alarms sounded, the PT men thought first of their boats, then of themselves. Any boat caught at the base, unprotected by camouflage, was at once manned and taken out, where if enemy bombs did fall she would at least have a fighting chance to dodge them.

At night the patrols continued.

"Some weird things happened on those patrols," Bob recalls. "Not important things, perhaps—not copy for the home-town headlines—but odd.

"For example. We were patrolling one night between Savo and Cape Esperance, everything quiet and most of the crew busy with sandwiches and coffee, when suddenly a flare broke out behind us. We turned to investigate. Chances were it was Maytag Charlie, who was always tossing out flares for the pure hell of it. But suddenly a brace of searchlights blinked on and began reaching around in the dark.

"We shut off the engines and lay quiet, and after a while the lights went out. Whoever he was, he'd probably heard the sound of our engines, though we were running muffled, and now, not finding us, he was convinced he'd been hearing things that didn't exist. We couldn't see him, and nothing else happened, so after sitting there a while we got under way again.

"Well, it wasn't long before Bill Kreiner nudged me and pointed off to starboard. In a whisper he said, 'Am I nuts, or do we have company?'

"He wasn't nuts. Out there a couple of hundred yards distant, something invisible was running along with us. We could hear the throb of its motors.

"I eased up on the throttle, but the sound stayed with us like an echo. I tried a burst of speed, but he wouldn't be shaken. At last I just couldn't stand it any longer. It was too much like one of those shudder-movies in which a fellow walks down a deserted street and keeps hearing footsteps behind him. 'What the hell,' I thought, 'this will go on forever!' So I swung the boat toward him.

LONG WERE THE NIGHTS

"Suddenly there were two silvery streaks in the water, heading straight for us. They were torpedoes, and there wasn't time to dodge. We just held our breaths and waited.

"The torpedoes passed right by us.

"We saw him then. At least we saw something low and dark on the surface, and knew what it was. It was a sub. Jap subs were not exactly rare in those waters—they came down rather often to hunt out our cargo ships—but this was our first encounter with one and we were startled. Before we got organized, he sent three more torpedoes at us. They, too, passed by the boat.

"So then we went for him. We barged in on him and fired two fish of our own, both of which missed. The Jap crash-dived and that ended it. We had no depth charges.

"But it was a close call for both the Jap and the PT boat. In all, five torpedoes had made tracks by us. When we ran off with mufflers closed a while later, every man aboard had his hand out for a cup of Mehes' coffee."

"Another time," Nick says, "the boat was on patrol between Kokumbona and Esperance. Nobody liked that beat. The men called it the 'Bitch Patrol.' You were all alone there, a couple of million miles from anything American, and if the enemy came down you were trapped between the incoming Japs and a section of Guadalcanal occupied by Jap troops in force.

"We used to wonder what would happen if anyone ran into trouble there—if, for instance, some of the boys had their boat shot out from under them and had to swim ashore where the Japs most certainly would be waiting with a reception committee. Nobody liked the idea of being a Jap prisoner, and some of the boys carried forty-fives, just in case.

"Forty-fives were a pretty good protection against sharks, as well. The accepted technique was to push the muzzle under water and pull the trigger; then if you were not lucky enough to hit the shark, the concussion would scare him away.

"On this particular night our boat and Tom Kendall's were creeping along fairly close together, on patrol off Kokumbona, when all at once Woodrow Wilson Cavanah, the lad with the auctioneer's voice, came up over Kendall's radio.

"'Niiick from Tawm!' he bawled. 'Theyuh's a landing barge awff yohre pawt bow!'

"I sang out the call to general quarters and looked for the barge but couldn't see it. John Legg and Crosson looked, too. We couldn't see a thing.

"'Ask him where!' I yelled at Pearle. 'Where is it?'

"'Awff yohre pawt bow!' retorted Cavanah. 'Look aout fohre it! Theyuh's a landing barge awff yohre pawt bow! We can still see it!' You'd have thought he was selling souvenirs at a circus.

"Aboard our boat we nearly went out of our minds. A landing barge! If the enemy had a barge there, it was our job to strafe him before he started shooting us up! But we couldn't see a thing—just Kendall's boat crawling along at slow speed a couple of hundred yards astern of us.

"At last, frantic, we radioed Tom to come up and give the Japs a going over—if he could still see them. And then came Cavanah's voice again, chanting the pay-off.

" 'Sawrry,' he said. 'We must have been lookin' at yohre wake awl the tyum! So saw-rry!'

"But you never know."

"You never do," says Bob. "Take the submarines, for instance. You never knew when one of those ugly customers would pop up and take a shot at you. Jack ran on a periscope wake one night—was on it before he saw it. Just a thin white line of bubbles in the water, and who would attach any threat of danger to a little thing like that, anyway?

"But the Jap was alert. He fired a torpedo and crash-dived. There wasn't a whole lot of room between the PT boat and that torpedo, and when the boys came in they were still having the jitters."

"Another time, one very dark night," Bob says, "Jack was feeling his way along at slow speed and came within fifty feet of ramming a Jap destroyer which was lying to off Savo. That's close; much too close. You can't fire a torpedo at that range; it hasn't time to arm itself and won't explode when it hits. Jack and the destroyer both turned away, with their machine-guns chattering.

"The Jap's gunners found the mark first that night and

poured their fire right into one of the PT's turrets. One of the bullets set off a belt of machine-gun cartridges under gunner Osborne's feet.

"It was a tough spot for Osborne—like being jammed into a tin can full of death-dealing wasps. That belt was leaping and lunging like a snake, exploding all over the place. And you know what that boy did? He reached down, picked up the exploding belt, threw it overside and went on firing.

"He did a thorough job on the Japs, too, before the PT was out of there."

These were the little things, small against the bigness of the overall picture but important to the men involved. Scarcely a night went by without some incident, some oddity, some outstanding act of courage on the part of one or more of the men.

On the night of November 10, many men were brave.

"Our orders that night," Nick reports, "were to go out and meet a force of enemy destroyers which had been seen on the way down from Bougainville. Three of us went out: Robbie, Tom Kendall, and our gang. Tom encountered the enemy first, southeast of Savo Island. Cavanah, 'the voice,' came up over the radio to inform the rest of us.

"It was an ugly night. We'd had a lot of rain and the sky was swollen with clouds that sat just over our heads, still dripping moisture. The Japs loved that kind of weather. We hated it. But on a PT boat you take what comes, and if the sea is rough, as this one was, you take that, too, with a

LONG WERE THE NIGHTS

deep breath every now and then to hold down the contents of your stomach. Don't let anyone dupe you into believing the PT boys were never seasick.

"Well, Cavanah sang out the Japs' disposition and speed, and the boats deployed for action. At a signal from Robbie we went on in. I pushed the PT in too fast, stirring up too much ocean, and the enemy saw our wake before we meant him to.

"All at once, dead ahead, a searchlight blazed on and the Japs started plastering all three boats.

"Searchlights are vicious things, and I'm sure that any man who has been blinded by one on a dark night, while closing for action, will back me up on that. As a rule you've been out there for some time before the action begins. You've been prowling about like a cat in a mine-shaft, getting accustomed to the dark, learning how to feel your way through it. In time you acquire a certain extrasensory vision, an ability to see things in the blackness.

"Then all at once, without warning, a dazzling light explodes against your eyes and all this night-conditioning becomes, instead of a blessing, a handicap. You feel as though the hair is being burned off your head, and you are the most conspicuous guy in the whole South Pacific area.

"That's what happened to us and to the other fellows when the Jap caught us in his lights. A moment later a second flood of light reached out for us from another ship off to port. Then both ships opened fire, and a salvo of 4.7s straddled our boat. Everything went black."

Nick does not know from first-hand observation what happened aboard his boat immediately after that. He was in a heap on the deck, dazed by the explosion, and had to piece the story together by questioning the crew later.

Many things did happen. Nick was out of it. Bernie O'Neill, the second in command, had been hurled against the side of the cockpit and was also out. The boat was growling forward on half-open throttles and the enemy destroyer dead ahead was concentrating all his fire in an effort to stop her.

The PT's crew lay strewn about the deck, some dazed and shaken, all of them rocked by the concussion. Some had been thrown against the torpedo tubes, others against the gun turrets. One man, aft, was spread-eagled over the 20-mm. Oerlikon, arms and legs asprawl. In the engine-room, conditions were much the same.

The first to get up was John Der, the lad with the bold, brilliant eagle on his chest. Der had been at his battle station beside the port tubes when the salvo hit. He got to his feet and clung to the tubes for support, shaking his head, dazedly looking around, trying to orient himself. Then he looked down at the tube on which he was leaning and saw the torpedo in it. Scrambling for his mallet, he whanged the percussion cap with all his might. The torpedo ran.

"I don't know why I did that," he confessed later. "The old bean was doing cartwheels, and when I saw the fish in the tube I remembered hearing a terrific racket just before

LONG WERE THE NIGHTS

the lights went out. First thing that flashed through my mind —the electric firing circuit must be on the fritz and we were having a hot run. That fish shouldn't be there. So I socked it."

He socked it and it sped straight as a plumb-line for the enemy destroyer ahead. The Jap was a broadside target, holding the speeding mosquito boat in his lights and hurling shells at her. Suddenly the dull red glow of a torpedo hit spread on his side underneath the bridge.

Aboard the PT, John Legg then got up. Legg had been close behind Nick when the Jap's fire raked the boat, and he was slammed against a turret. He found his feet and saw that the boat was closing the destroyer.

Legg stumbled to the wheel and got his hands on it. Bleeding and dazed, he swung the boat around and pushed the throttles up against the windshield, to begin a perfectly executed retirement.

Leon Nale was up. He had been in one of the 50-caliber turrets and the concussion had hurled him to the deck of the tank room below. Now, struggling, he picked himself up and dragged himself back into the turret. Looking around in a fog, he saw Legg at the wheel, Der at the torpedo tube. A shell cracked overhead and he ducked. Enemy fire was thick as rain and the night was striped with tracers. Nale braced himself.

Wedged there, still only half conscious, he swung the fifty's twin snouts into position and began blazing away at the enemy's searchlights.

That was when Nick came to.

"Bernie and I," Nick says, "were both trying to make sense enough to get to the wheel and throttles, and hadn't a very clear idea of what had happened, although we did know we were in trouble. The boat was in the midst of her turn, with Legg at the helm and the Jap so close aboard that I was looking almost straight up into his lights. The next thing I knew, Nale got the range and the lights went out.

"Crosson came to then. Always prompt on the trigger, he sized up the situation very quickly and, without waiting for a command, made a bee-line for the smoke generator. Der ran to help him, and they opened up the smoke. Down below, Porterfield went to work with Carner on the engines. With Legg still at the wheel, we conducted a successful retirement. But it took quick thinking and courage on the part of every enlisted man on the boat to make that escape."

About this time, one of the men popped his head from the mouth of the empty torpedo tube. His job finished, he had ducked in there for cover. The rest of the crew stared at him in amazement.

How he had managed to wriggle in there was a mystery. He was a little guy and that helped, but to shinny out to the end of a torpedo tube and slide down into it with the boat bucking heavy seas at top speed, a man would have to be half Houdini and half mountain-goat! This lad had done it. They saw him crawl out.

He grinned at them and gave his tube an affectionate pat.

Said one of the astonished crew: "What the Sam Hill were you doing in there?"

Replied the agile one very calmly: "Hell, you guys didn't need me any more"—which was true—"and if you know any safer place on this glorified egg-crate, just lead me to it. At least these tubes aren't plywood!" And with a flip of his hand he vanished below.

The boat was in the clear and running, her part of the action over. At the radio, Owen Pearle sent out the word on the enemy disposition, as the PT headed for home. Thanks to John Der's proficiency with the mallet, she had a hit on an enemy destroyer to her credit.

Meanwhile Kendall's boat was conducting a swift retirement, too. Carl Todd, the cook, was out of his galley and manning one of the guns that night, and explained later the reason for his boat's hasty retreat. "It wasn't the Japs we were scared of," he said. "It was you guys. When you turned away from that destroyer, you were like a bunch of barroom drunks on a toot. If we'd hung around another minute you'd have sunk *us!*"

Hugh Robinson had fired a spread of torpedoes into the heart of the enemy formation while the Japs were hurling their fire at him. Hugh's boat was not given credit for sinking a Jap—credit was always difficult to obtain unless the enemy was actually seen to sink—but at least one of her torpedoes found a mark and a Jap destroyer blew up with a loud, long roll of thunder. Then the PT ran for home.

"Just incidentally" the Japs did, too.

LONG WERE THE NIGHTS

For their heroism that night, two of Nikoloric's crew were singled out by those in authority. Leon Nale received honorary advancement in rating for his proficiency in shooting out the lights of the enemy destroyer while the little thunder boat beneath him was flying through a fast turn. John Legg was awarded the Silver Star for his handling of the boat during the critical moments.

But the entire crew had proved its mettle in those frightening seconds when the PT roared headlong toward destruction. "Every one of them," Nick says humbly, "came through with flying colors, and when I erect my own little monument to heroism, the name of every man aboard will be on it. They knew what to do and did it—did it so well that the lives of all of us were saved. I can't forget for a minute that I was among the last to get my wits back, and if the boys had not done what they did *before* that happened, I would not be here to tell about it.

"As Bernie O'Neill said with heartfelt enthusiasm when it was all over: 'What a crew! Boy, what a crew!'"

Chapter Eight

"SHOES?" said the Marine, eyeing Nick's feet. "You want some shoes? Whatsamatter with the ones you got?"

Nick looked at his feet, too, and said, "Well, for one thing they're worn out. The mud gets through them. I go around with wet feet all the time."

"Well, I'll tell you," the Marine said. "There's a guy over at the hospital was luggin' an extra pair of shoes when they brought him in." He told Nick the man's name. "Maybe he'll be feelin' good and let you have 'em."

Nick went over to the hospital. He had not come to Tulagi village to acquire a pair of shoes, but he needed them and if there was a chance of finding a pair he could not afford to pass it up. At the hospital he talked to a number of Marines who had been brought over from Guadalcanal. Some had been nicked by Jap snipers and some were victims of malaria and dysentery. Others were suffering from Guadalcanal Sickness, which was a malaise more complex and prevalent than all the others combined.

These were the men who had reached the breaking point in their struggle to remain sane under conditions no human nerves were designed to endure. They were brave enough; no one questioned their courage. In combat they had hurled back the fanatical Japs time and again with grisly losses. But the sleepless nights, the heat and rain and insects, the apparent hopelessness of their situation and the growing belief that help might never come, had worn them out.

They had lost weight. Some were forty pounds lighter than when they had first stormed ashore to meet the enemy. Their nerves were so taut that the smallest alien sound caused them to jump in alarm. Interludes of mental blackout were frequent, when some could not recall their names. Their hands shook, heads ached.

Worst of all were those who mistakenly blamed themselves for not being able to "take it" and sat silently by themselves, looking into space. Brave men, all of them—but ill.

Nick's man looked up at him and said quietly, "Sure, Mac. I got some real lucky shoes you can have." He reached under his cot for them and pulled them out—Marine issue shoes with heavy rubber soles; just the thing for gripping a PT's bouncing deck.

"A guy in my outfit—buddy of mine—wore 'em," the Marine said. "He was in the first wave that hit the beach August 7, and later on he fought at the Tenaru River and the Matanikau. He was out the night we gave the Japs hell on Bloody Hill, too. He always wore these shoes. He got a bunch of Japs."

Nick took the shoes and tried them for size. His feet were snug in them.

"What happened to this fellow?" Nick asked.

"He left the shoes in camp one time. We found him dead next day in front of a Jap machine-gun nest."

LONG WERE THE NIGHTS

Nick put on the lucky shoes and threw his own worn-out footwear away. He went back to the PT base, and it was nice to be able to walk along Main Street, on Snob Hill, without feeling the mud oozing up between his toes.

An accident occurred about this time which put two of the PT boats out of commission. Out on patrol together one night were Stilly Taylor and Bob Searles. It began to rain, and in the darkness the boats lost contact with each other.

It rained harder. Before long the night was a descending flood with visibility reduced to zero.

Suddenly Stilly saw a blurred shape in the darkness ahead, and spun his wheel to clear it. There was a tearing crash. The boat shuddered and shook herself. The men picked themselves up and saw what had happened.

They had rammed the other boat in the dark, gouging a hole eight feet long in her plywood hull. The bow, when they shook her free, was a blunted mass of splinters.

Limping homeward through the rain, both boats barely managed to make port.

But Squadron "X" had the men to attend to such troubles. At the base on Tulagi, Earl Wallace and Ed Olsen had put together a carpenter shop in which minor miracles occurred daily. Already they had very nearly finished rebuilding the bow of Robbie's boat, which had been hit by enemy shellfire November 7. With surgeon's skill they had cut away the fragments of the wound and were fitting a completely new bow which when finished would look and be as good as new. Now they rolled up their sleeves and went to work as well on the newly damaged boats.

"Without those two men," says Bob, "we never in this world would have kept the boats running. They literally wore themselves out to hold the squadron together, and their shop was the most amazing place on the island."

Wallace and Olsen had other headaches, too. New members were continually being enrolled in the "Hard Rock Club"—an organization reserved for those whose boats had run on uncharted coral reefs. There was nothing exclusive about the Hard Rock Club. By now it included almost everyone. But Olsen and Wallace took it in stride. Without complaint they went to work on the boats' bottoms and put them right again.

Others at the base were equally tireless. Lorran Beed and Arthur Stuffert worked day and night to keep the engines in shape. Wing and O'Daniel sweated over the torpedoes. Storekeeper Golden was a walking warehouse of stores and equipment. Doc Perkins built a sick bay and hovered tirelessly over an increasing number of malaria patients. Charlie Tufts ran the base by day and rode the boats by night.

But for all their efforts, the squadron was not in the best of shape when the enemy made his next major bid to retake Guadalcanal. Nightly patrols had again worn ragged the nerves of the men and reduced the efficiency of crews and boats alike.

Robbie's boat, not quite finished, was still in the carpenter shop. Two others were laid up for collision repairs. Only five of the eight boats were left, and despite herculean work these were sluggish and temperamental.

On November 12 began the all-out battle which in the opinion of many experts decided the fate of the Solomons campaign. The navy refers to it as the Battle of Guadalcanal. Squadron "X" was a part of it.

For some time now, heavy American and Japanese naval forces in the Solomons area had been exchanging blows, many of them violent but none decisive. There had been a number of major actions and many minor ones, and some bitter engagements between sea and air forces. The enemy had managed to put ashore some troops. Now the struggle was reaching its climax both at sea and ashore.

Intelligence had known for some time that the enemy was massing his naval strength for something tremendous. Patrol planes had been sweeping out of Guadalcanal in a steady stream, fighting their way through heavy weather to the northwest to find out what was brewing. Scuttlebutt was rife on both Guadalcanal and Tulagi, and the ground forces on the islands were uneasy. This time the Japs apparently intended to throw in everything they possessed.

On November 11, in a race to build up strength to meet the expected onslaught, American transports began landing reinforcements on Guadalcanal. The operation continued through November 12, while army and Marine pilots battled enemy planes in the bloody skies above and a naval task force under Rear Admiral Daniel J. Callaghan stood by to keep the sea-lanes safe.

LONG WERE THE NIGHTS

The Japs did all they could to prevent the move, but failed. One of their bombers, dying from a burst of anti aircraft fire, plummeted to the deck of the cruiser *San Francisco*, in one of the war's cruelest minor tragedies. Eighteen of the *San Francisco's* men were killed and many others injured when the plane exploded.

That night Admiral Callaghan met an invasion force off Savo Island and, pitting destroyers and cruisers against the enemy's heaviest armor, put the Japs to rout. The encounter was a point-blank affair at the height of which enemy fire raked the bridge of the American flagship and killed both Admiral Callaghan and Captain Young, the ship's commander.

The Japs retired. All the next day, November 13, they lay in hiding among their island bases. When night fell, units of the reorganized enemy fleet moved in again.

"Over at PT headquarters," Bob recalls, "we were standing around waiting for orders, and were told that a force of six destroyers and a battleship or heavy cruiser was on the way down. It might be a feeler force; it might be the beginning of another climax try to take the island. At any rate the Japs were again on the move, and our orders were to get out there and be useful. So out we went."

The five boats in commission that night were skippered by Les Gamble, Bob Searles, Jack Searles, Tom Kendall and Stilly Taylor. They were given a fine cover of darkness and their method of attack was much like that used on the night of the PTs' first engagement, when Lieutenant Commander Montgomery had led them. Five abreast, they moved at sneak-in speed toward the enemy's probable position.

A heavy responsibility was theirs, and they were fully aware of it. Unless Intelligence had made a mistake, this enemy force was not the main show but a reconnaissance unit, designed to determine, if possible, how much of the available American strength had been whittled down in the previous nights' engagements. If this feeler force could be hit hard and disorganized, the Japs conceivably might be persuaded to change their plans. If not, all hell would certainly erupt before many more hours had passed.

"Failing to establish contact," says Bob, "we split into two groups. The first three boats—Jack, Tom and myself—lay in wait for the Japs off Sandfly Passage, to attack them on the way in. We had to wait about half an hour.

"They were moving fast when they came, and were hard to see in the dark because they were not yet shelling the island and we had no gun-flashes to guide us. Each of us fired four torpedoes. Something was wrong with our estimate of the enemy's speed, and we scored no hits.

"But though we were bitterly disappointed, it turned out that we had really set the stage for the other two boats. Because when the Japs finally swung into position and began to shell the island, they apparently thought there was nothing more to fear from the PTs. The first thing they did was put up some flares to guide their gunners.

"Stilly Taylor was there waiting, and with him was Jack

who, after firing his own torpedoes, had raced down ahead of the Japs to get aboard with Les Gamble. The enemy's flares guided the two PTs, and the boats moved in to attack.

"Stilly went in first. By the light of the flares he and his crew made out seven ships clearly, one of them big enough to be a battleship. Later reports said it was a cruiser. At any rate, the PT picked it for a target and fired a spread at a little over a thousand yards. The other boat concentrated on the destroyers.

"The Japs didn't blink an eye until those torpedoes hit them. They had even put up more flares. Then, of course, it was too late for them to act. The two PTs were out of there with empty tubes, on their way back to the barn.

"Behind them the big ship was ablaze from a hit, and one of the screening destroyers was exploding into a pyre of smoke and flames. The destroyer sank, and the whole enemy force turned back.

"Actually, it was an easy attack for the motor torpedo boats. The flashes of gunfire had made a perfect target as the boats moved in for the kill, and the enemy ships could fire only a few wild rounds as the PTs fled for their base. But those two mosquito boats saved our men and planes on Henderson Field from catching a lot of hell that night. The torpedo hits broke up what started to be an intensified shelling, calculated to soften up our forces for the big all-out blitz the Japs were planning for the next night."

Actually, too, the hit scored by Stilly Taylor on the enemy cruiser resulted in its destruction and was responsible for the sinking of a second Jap cruiser. In returning to their base, the Japs were forced to reduce their speed to a crawl, to enable the crippled ship to keep pace with them. From Bougainville, at dawn, a second cruiser sped down to assist them, and the entire force was surprised by Guadalcanal planes a short time later—planes which might not have been able to fly at all had not Stilly and Jack broken up the shelling party. These planes concentrated their attack on the two cruisers and sank them. Only the destroyers escaped.

But the enemy was still not discouraged. He had assembled the most powerful force of warships ever brought together in the South Pacific, and despite severe wounds, the great sprawling hulk of that fleet was still intact. All that day it covered the sea like a fat, slow-moving slug, pushing ever closer to Guadalcanal despite the jabbing, stabbing attacks of American planes.

Marines and newly arrived army reinforcements on the island entrenched themselves on the beaches to repel the expected assault. At dusk the enemy monster was closing in, bloody but persistent, and as darkness fell it struck again.

On Tulagi, PT Squadron "X" nervously awaited orders. Only three of its eight boats were ready for service. Those which had been out the previous night were still being rearmed with torpedoes—a long, hard job which took time. Brent Greene, Nick and Robbie were the skippers of the three boats in commission. Robbie was in charge.

"The senior naval officer on Tulagi at that time," Nick recalls, "was Lieutenant Commander John Alderman, skipper of the *McFarland*. When we reported in at six o'clock to find out what was expected of us, he was very grave.

" 'I don't know what you fellows can do,' the commander said to us, 'but I suppose you ought to get out there and try to do it, anyway.' He was a quiet man, thin and tanned, and something was obviously troubling him. We thought we knew what it was, because it was bothering us, too—if such a mild word is adequate to describe a kind of semi-paralysis which gives you the jumping jitters and causes cold sweat to break out like a rash all over you.

"This troublesome 'something' was the suspicion we all had that our navy had gone off somewhere on some job the front office may have considered more vital than the defense of Guadalcanal and Tulagi. With so much going on, communications were badly choked up and most of us on Tulagi were totally in the dark about what was really happening. It's possible the *McFarland's* skipper was in the dark, too—though none of us asked him in so many words.

"At any rate, he looked at us long and quietly, shook hands and said, 'Good luck.' Then he added, almost as an afterthought: 'Your job is to slip through the escorting warships, if you can, and get the transports. Unless, of course, you receive word to retire.'

"Robbie, our squadron commander, wet his lips and said we would do our best. The rest of us wondered just how good our best would be, against that kind of opposition. Because—good God!—the whole Jap navy was on the way, and we were just three little torpedo boats!"

LONG WERE THE NIGHTS

The PT men, not saying much, returned to their boats and began to ready them for action, fervently hoping there was some truth in the rumor they had heard that Admiral Lee was around somewhere with a force of American warships. They wondered if those warships were on the way and if so, would they arrive in time. Because if they didn't, there would be little left of Squadron "X" when the action was over. The PTs might sink some Japs—might even disrupt the enemy's plans for a while—but if any of the midget mosquito boats came back from the engagement, it would be a miracle.

At the base, the enlisted men were glum with misgivings, too. They had heard some of the radio reports. They had intercepted some of the Marine scuttlebutt, too. Now they plagued the officers with questions.

How big was the Jap? Where was the U. S. fleet? What time would the enemy be in? Was it "the works" this time or just another prelude? Were the PT boats being sent out to face that kind of opposition *alone?* What about Lee?

"Ain't he the guy fought over there in China? Calls himself Ching Chong Lee?" someone asked.

"That's him. He's all right."

"We sure could use him. No kiddin', we sure could use him now."

"For God's sake, skipper, give us the dope. Tell us what's up!"

"But," says Nick, "we didn't give them the dope. Not all of it. We simply didn't have the heart. These boys had fought with us night after night and they were the grandest guys on earth. I, for one, owed my life to the men on my boat. We couldn't tell them they were going out there to be expended. We just couldn't do it. But most of them knew it, anyway."

The three mosquito boats cleared Tulagi harbor and spread out, maintaining radio contact—three motor torpedo boats deployed against a Jap force of unknown but certainly tremendous size, including at least two big battleships, eight to ten cruisers, twenty or more transports and probably a score of destroyers. It was a black hour for the PT boats. The men knew well enough what they were up against, and few of them failed to show it. Tense, quiet, they stood at battle stations while the three boats crept stealthily through the dark. They had faced the Japs before, these men. They knew and respected the enemy's ability. Against the Bougainville Express they had done well. But tonight they faced the bulk of the enemy's South Pacific fleet.

"I, for one," Nick confesses, "was doing a lot of sober thinking about little far-away things not at all connected with the defense of Guadalcanal. I was scared stiff."

It was about ten o'clock when Hugh Robinson saw the advance guard of the oncoming enemy horde. He and his crew made out the blurred, creeping shadows of a score or more of ships, and the radioman, Gavin Hamilton, sent out the word—"Here they are, gang!"—with no attempt to lighten its significance. Hamilton was an old-timer, fond of telling the men about his folks back home in Alabama. He must have been thinking very hard about the home folks then.

"The Japs," Nick reports, "were coming down west of Savo Island, and when the word came from Robbie we turned out to be in position to attack. It wasn't long before we and Brent Greene's crew saw them, too—a screen of destroyers so numerous that they looked like black bees pouring out of a hive. Behind the destroyers were the bigger, more powerful capital ships in tight formation.

"Apparently the transports, which we'd been ordered to try to get, were in back of this advancing force of warships, and so there was but one course of attack open to us. It was the hard course. We had to go through the warships."

The three PTs warily advanced, feeling for an opening in the huge enemy fleet. On all three boats the men were unnaturally quiet. John Der's tattooed eagle was not screaming defiance at the Japs now. Legg was not concerned with the intricacies of navigation. The machinist's mates checked their engines for that impending moment when speed and speed alone would be the boats' only salvation.

They spoke in whispers, all of them, when they spoke at all. There was none of the customary give-and-take of side talk, even though silence was not essential to safety. Gilpin, inveterate Southerner, was not re-fighting the Civil War now. Lee Bagby's thoughts were not on mathematics, nor Stevens' on the problems of Snob Hill. Jake Kearney, eagle-eyed exec on Brent Greene's boat, remembered college days at Alabama and wondered if he would ever again see Fifty-second Street.

Gilpin sat taut at the radio, hunched forward a little, his hands covering the phones at his ears. Owen Pearle waited, too. At any moment the word would come from Robbie—the last word, perhaps, that these men, brave and skillful but now about to be expended against hopeless odds, might ever hear and obey.

It came. The voice was Robbie's own. "All right, gang," he said. "Let's give it a try."

Brent Greene looked at Kearney and nodded. He pushed up the throttles. More swiftly, but still with speed in reserve for the moment when enemy searchlights would pin her down, the PT moved through the dark toward that sprawling mass of enemy shadows. The other boat, too, growled forward.

And then up over the radio came another voice, a voice the PT men had never heard before. Loud, sure of itself, with just a trace of habitual good humor, it boomed out through the speakers to the men aboard the thunder boats.

"Boys, this is Ching Chong Lee! Did you ever hear of me?"

The PT men caught their breath. Goddard let out a whoop and turned a handspring on the deck of his boat. Leon Nale voiced a howl of glee. Over the radio came Robbie's elated reply—a rush of words which told plainly how he and his men were feeling.

LONG WERE THE NIGHTS

"Yes, sir! We sure have!"

"Then get those boats the hell out of the way! I'm coming through!" the admiral replied.

Somehow or other without making any sound that could have been heard by the Japs, the men managed to cheer themselves hoarse. They were kids on a picnic. Greene, Robbie and Nick swung their boats around and were wearing grins as broad as their faces as they pushed the throttles up. The little boats belched out a thunderous, thankful roar and went winging wide open for regions of lesser peril.

The PTs retired about three miles, which their skippers thought would be far enough to place them out of range, yet close enough to insure a front-row seat for the show. There, with engines silent, they sat tight. The engine-room crews came on deck.

Coffee and sandwiches were passed up from the galleys, and the men made themselves comfortable on gun turrets or torpedo tubes. Like kids at a circus they sat waiting for the elephants.

"When they came," Nick says, "the elephants were not so numerous as we had expected. We learned later that his battleships were armed with sixteen-inch guns, which is more than the Japs had, but in numbers the enemy had odds of four or five to one. It looked like deliberate suicide.

"But we remembered the admiral's voice, yelling at us over the radio to get the hell out of there, and we somehow felt very sure that he knew what he was doing."

Lee's force had come up from the south, skirting the western shore of Guadalcanal. Approaching Savo Island, the destroyers hung back. The two battleships made a complete circuit of the little island and took up positions in the channel between Savo and Guadalcanal.

When the Japs rounded Savo, bound for the Guadalcanal beachhead to form a screen for their following transports, Lee was waiting like a two-headed spider in the mouth of its tunnel.

"When the battle-wagons opened fire," Nick says, "we on the PT boats looked at each other uneasily and said, 'This is it.' But if we still had any doubts about Admiral Lee's chances, they began to be dissipated about thirty seconds later. The big guns on the battleships bellowed in unison, three turrets on each, and the very first salvo burst like an earthquake in the midst of three Jap ships.

"One Jap simply disintegrated. Another burst into a roaring column of flames which lit up the scene for yards around, red and unreal as a bad painting, until the flames were engulfed in a climbing cone of dense black smoke. The remaining Jap opened fire and sent up a spread of star shells which went wobbling crazily across the sky; then the battleships' guns let loose another angry roar and Jap number three went up in a spurt of flame.

"The whole action took about six minutes, maybe a little more. Our battleships then swung north toward us, and we could see the flagship quite clearly against the background of smoky light thrown up by the burning Japs. There were no star shells now. The quarter moon, clear and high, threw a kind of mystic haze over everything, turning ships to shadows. Out beyond us, northwest of Savo, a second battle was raging, and apparently our destroyers were in the thick of it.

"You had to look two ways at once then, and we were like spectators at a tennis match, twisting our necks first one way, then the other. Our destroyers were giving and catching hell to port, and off to starboard a big Jap cruiser was tearing around on some crazy maneuver like a fish without a tail. Either he was in a great big hurry to get out of there with a whole skin, or he hoped to lead Admiral Lee's two battle-wagons into some sort of trap.

"The admiral wasn't having any. All at once the turrets of one of our battleships split the night wide open again, with a racket that must have been heard in Australia, and three blazing globes of fire sped from the ship's guns. It was a strange, awesome sight. The three red globes left the guns in a blurred streak, soaring up and up as though reaching for the moon, and then very slowly they fell seaward again. The maneuvering Jap burst into flames.

"Again and again those triplet balls of fire looped across the sky, and when they fell, the Jap was always under them. At last he stopped running. The flames had engulfed him. He sat there, burning like a bonfire, until a pall of smoke spread out to smother him.

"Out beyond Savo, meanwhile, the grimmest kind of fighting was going on. We were not close enough to identify the ships—or even, for that matter, to see them except for the gun-flashes and the glare of burning vessels—but later we learned that our four destroyers had engaged two or three times their number of enemy destroyers, plus a Jap heavy cruiser, and were slugging it out toe to toe. The navy said two of our destroyers were lost. We saw them burning. But at least four other ships were in flames, too.

"Then one of our battleships took a hand, and the devastation was tremendous. All over the sea ships were exploding and bursting into flames.

"On our boat the boys were mute with wonder. Some still clutched their coffee cups, the coffee cold and forgotten. One of them—Parrish, I think—had squeezed a sandwich so hard that the tuna-fish was oozing out between his fingers.

"Alvis, a navy man from 'way back who had been around and seen plenty of other hair-raising sights, kept saying, 'My God, I can't believe it! I never saw anything like it! My God, it's tremendous!'"

About that time, one of Admiral Lee's battleships ran into trouble. The Japs had pinned her with searchlights. First two blinding beams of light stabbed at her, then two more, all of them from a Jap ship which was one of three huge shadows emerging from the darker, lumpier shadow of Savo Island.

"The Japs opened fire and our battleship answered," Nick says, "and we saw those three red balls again, so lazy in flight that you thought you could hit them with a twenty-two. At the same time a lot of smaller stuff, secondary batteries, went into action and jammed the night with noise.

"The lights were shot out and more came on. Then one of the Japs, a cruiser, blew up and broke in halves with flames pouring from it as though each half were trying to destroy the other with giant flame-throwers. It painted the scene a bright, brilliant red, through which more of those soaring red balls fell seaward. A second Jap cruiser blew up and broke in two. It was unbelievable.

"Alvis kept saying hoarsely, 'My God! My God!' All the men felt the same. No one could think of anything really intelligent to say until later, when it was all over, and then we spoke in queerly stilted phrases, like a lot of strangers trying timidly to impress one another at first meeting. The immensity of the thing had stunned us—the awful noise and confusion, the flames and smoke and the sight of big ships being smashed as though by some power beyond human control. There were men on those ships. Thousands of men. There was massive, expensive machinery. And suddenly instead of any of those things there would be only a vast, earthquake roar and an erupting volcano of destruction.

"Of course we couldn't make out the details of the action. Most of those we got later, from the men on the battle-wagons. But we could tell that somebody was taking a tremendous licking, and we were all pretty positive that it wasn't Admiral Lee or Captain Gatch.

"But it was not over yet. There was one final action—between the second of our battleships and the last of those big Jap ships in the shadow of Savo. Savo's shadow was a crimson haze now from the two Japs already burning, and Admiral Lee was pounding the last Jap with everything he had.

"We couldn't keep track of the number of times the Jap was hit. We tried, but after each explosion we'd say, "That's it; that has to be it!'—and he'd still be there, feebly returning our battleship's fire. He exploded until there was simply nothing left of him to blow up. Literally he was hammered to pieces, and his last hopeless counter-fire was from a turret completely enveloped in flames.

"That ended it. The Battle of Guadalcanal was over. The whole show had lasted perhaps an hour. None of us had ever before seen anything like it, or expected to again. There simply was nothing left of the enormous Jap fleet which had steamed in so confidently just a short time before. Our side had lost two destroyers. The Jap had lost nearly everything.

"And Squadron 'X' had not been expended after all."

Tulagi Island, where the PT's were based, on the left. Florida Island is in the background. *(U.S. National Archives)*

"Iron-Bottom Sound", the scene of much of the action in this book, with Savo Island in the background. *(U.S. National Archives)*

PT boat ferries captured Japanese prisoners from Florida Island to Guadalcanal. *(Photo courtesy of Lester Gamble)*

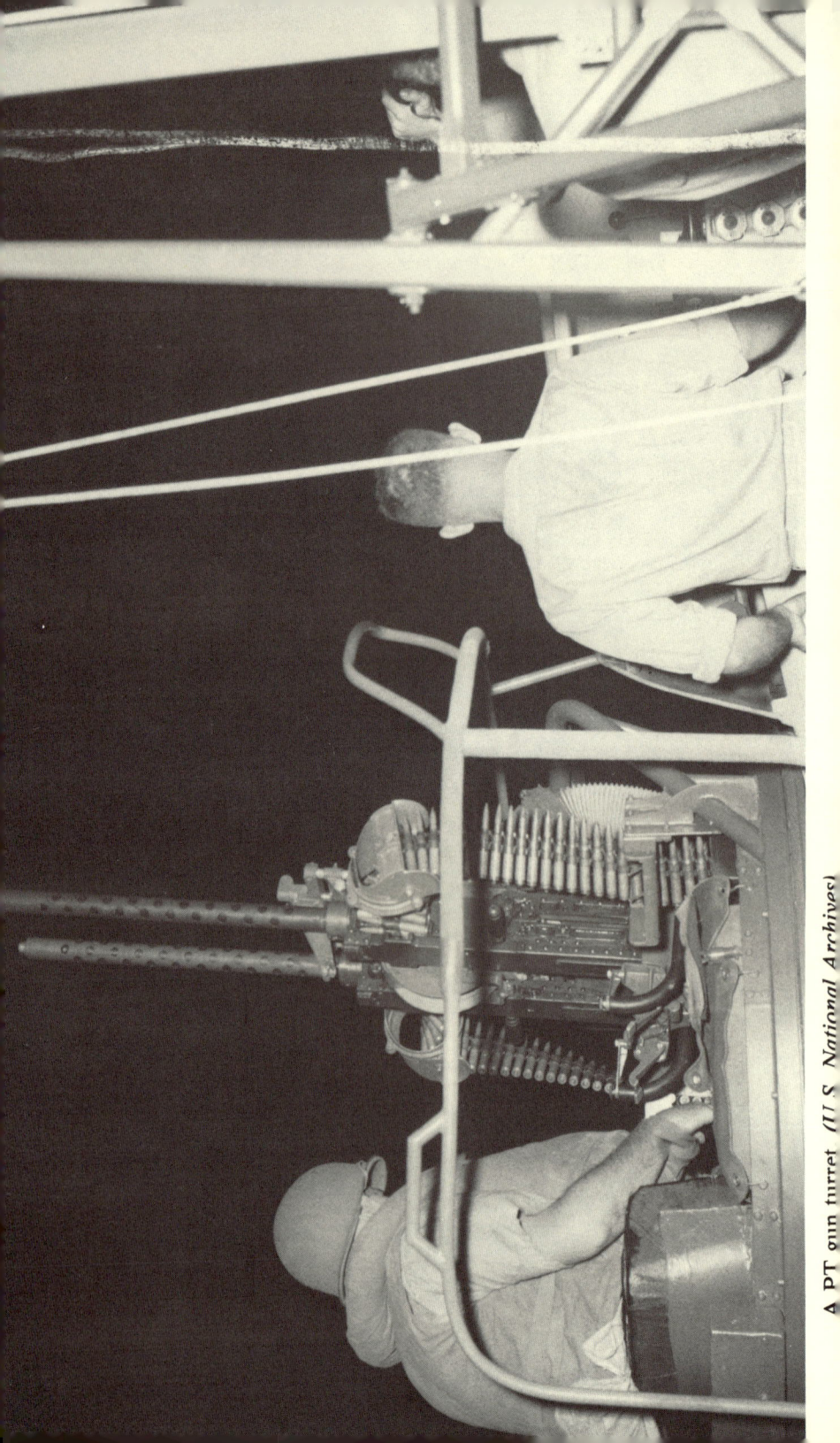

A PT gun turret. (U.S. National Archives)

Lt. Hugh Robinson, on right, and Lt. (jg.) Les Gamble after Guadalcanal was secured. *(Photo courtesy of Lester Gamble)*

Lt. (jg.) L. Nikoloric, Lt. (jg.) J. Kernell, and Lt. H.S. Taylor, left to right, pose with natives on Tulagi in November 1942. *(Photo courtesy of Joseph Kernell)*

Lt. (jg.) Les Gamble, on left, and Ens. Bart Connolly in front of sleeping hut on Florida Island. *(Photo courtesy of Lester Gamble)*

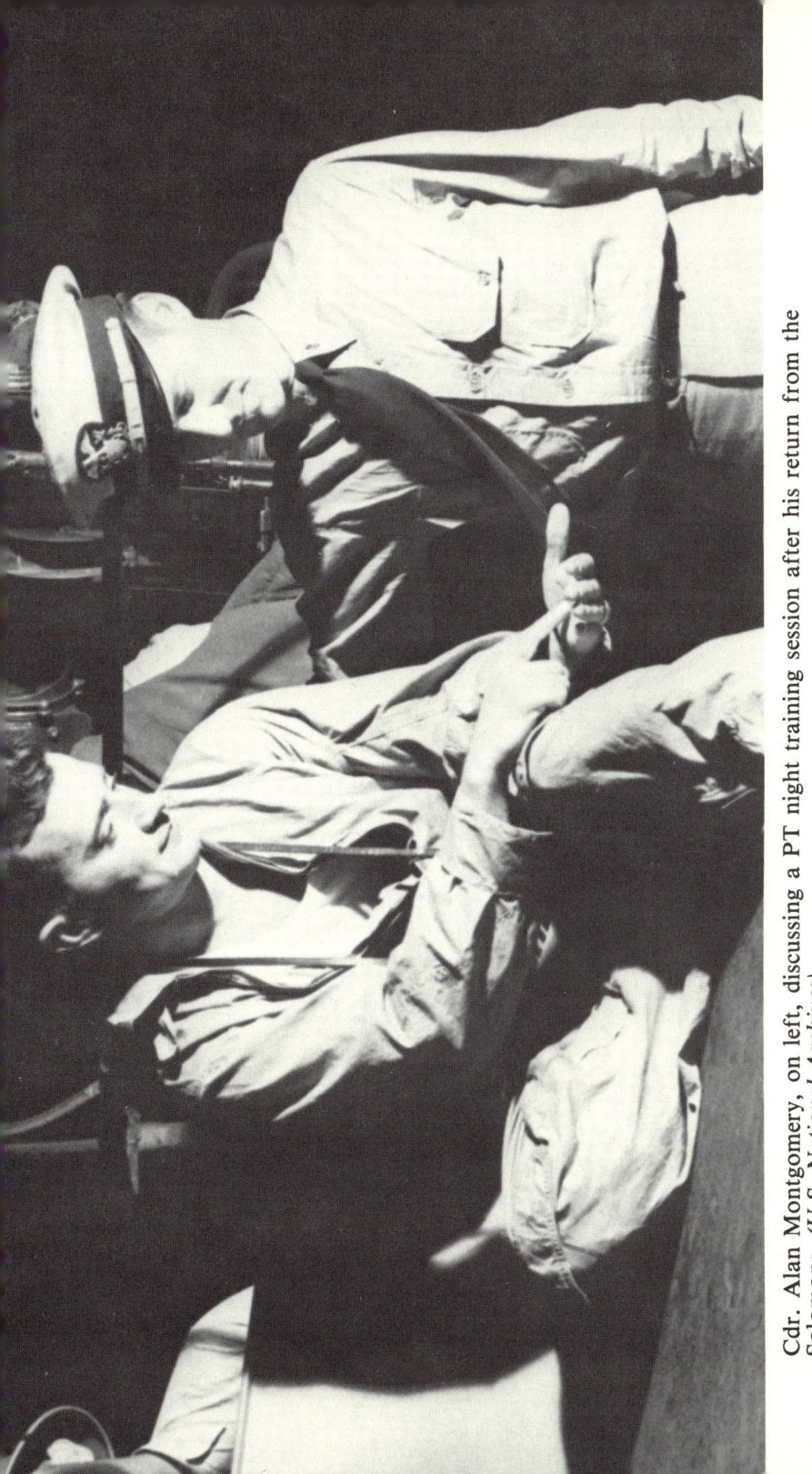

Cdr. Alan Montgomery, on left, discussing a PT night training session after his return from the Solomons. (*U.S. National Archives*)

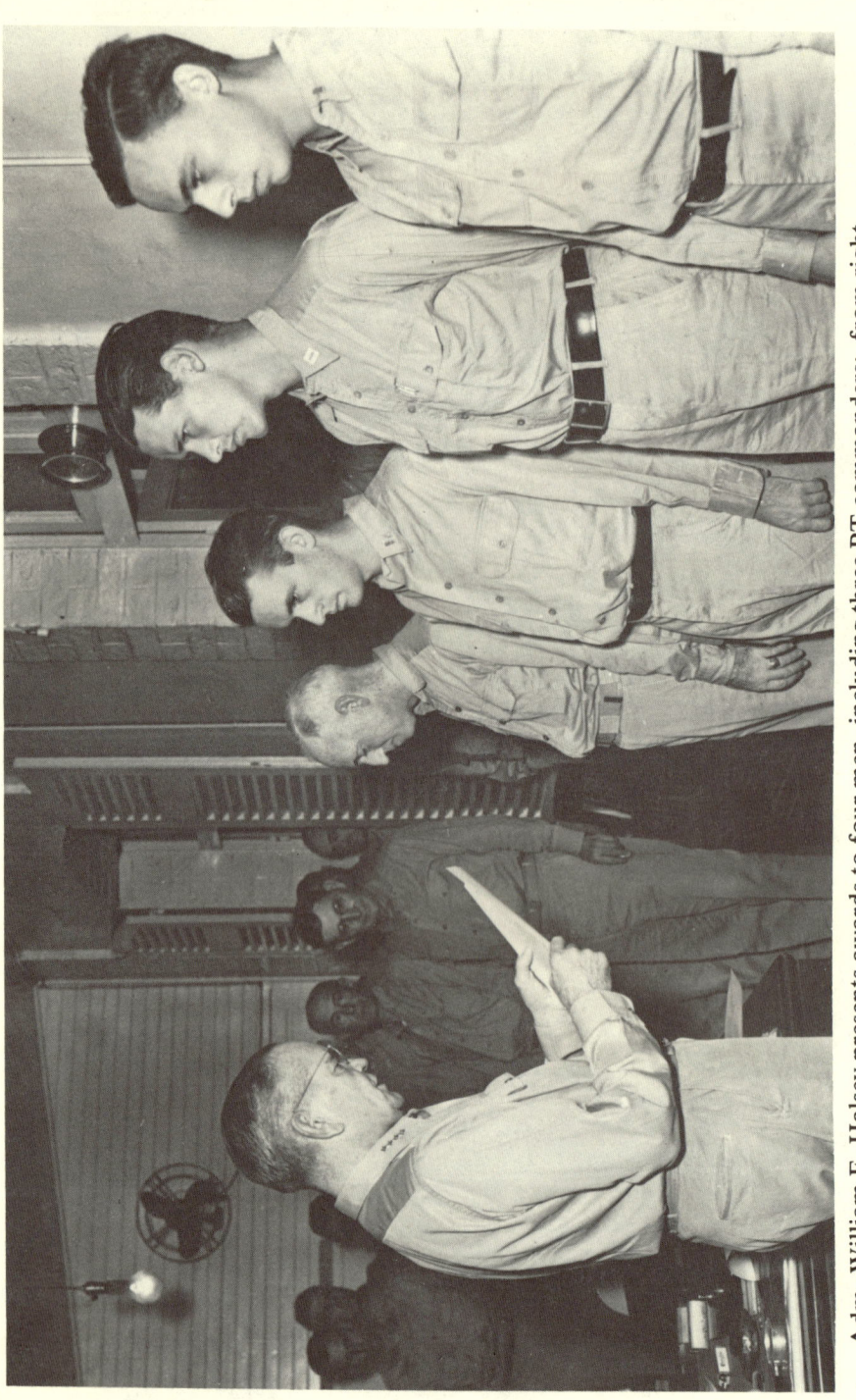

Adm. William F. Halsey presents awards to four men, including three PT commanders: from right, Lt. (jg.) L.A. Nikoloric, Lt. H.S. Taylor and Lt. R.L. Searles. *(U.S. National Archives)*

A PT boat and crew is saved from the gunfire of a Jap destroyer by the smoke screen from the PT's smoke generator.

A Jap destroyer feels the sting of a PT's torpedo.

A PT crew helps rescue survivors of the cruiser *Northampton*.

A PT crew member frantically works to fix smoke generator as Jap ship fires on PT boat.

Jap submarine torpedo narrowly misses a PT boat.

A PT's torpedoes about to score a hit on a Jap submarine.

A Jap destroyer catches a PT in the glare of its searchlight.

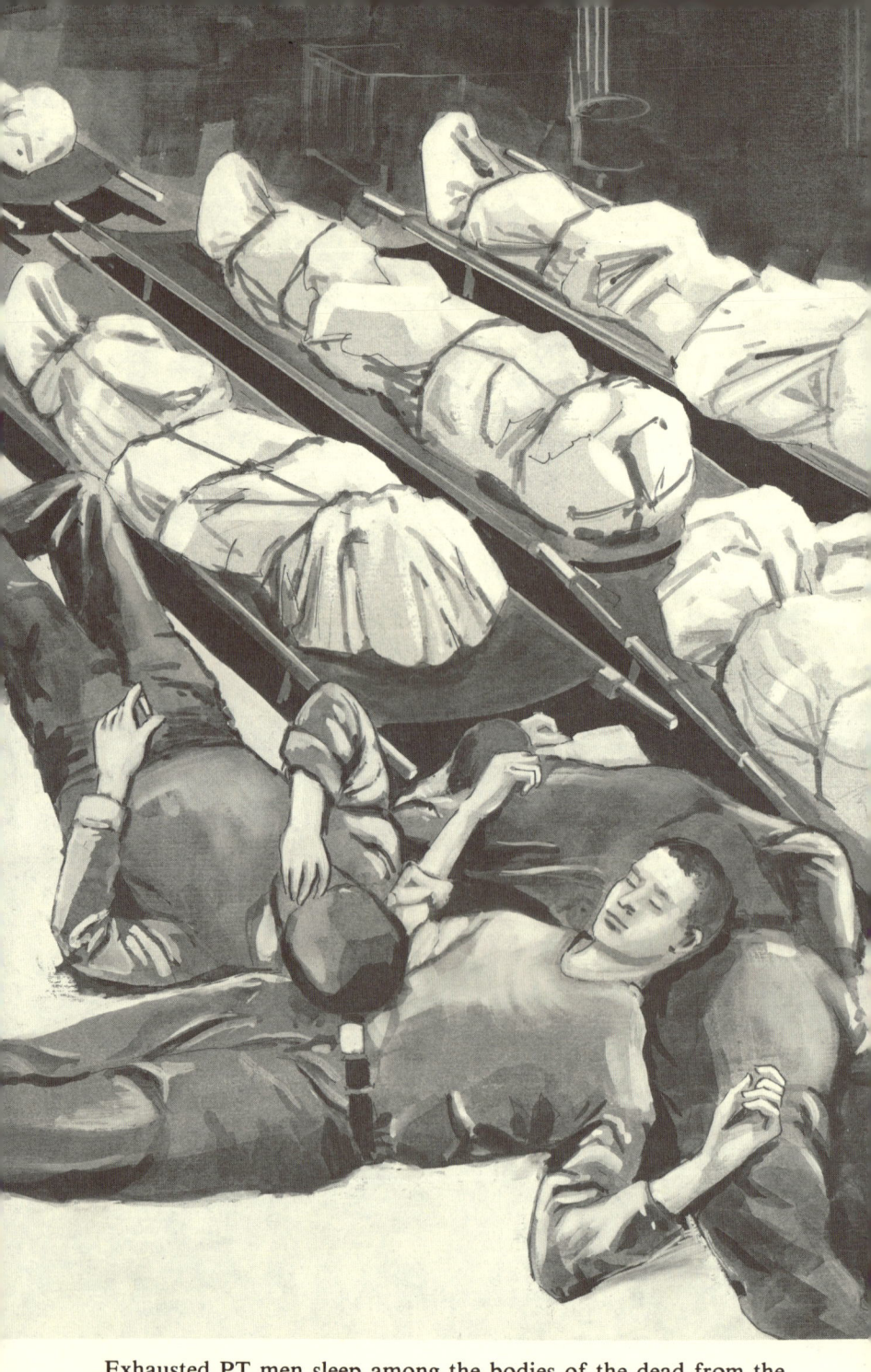

Exhausted PT men sleep among the bodies of the dead from the destroyer *McFarland*.

Chapter Nine

Cotton and Coberth were sweating over engines at the base. The day was a broiler. The two machinist's mates were stripped to their pants, smeared with oil and grease, and when either of them stopped work for a moment to wipe the moisture from his eyes with the back of a grimy hand, the oil and grease were transferred to his face in streaks of war-paint.

Chief yeoman Wicks came by and paused to grin at them. "You fellows better watch out," he said, "or some of the natives will mistake you for kinfolk and hustle you off."

Chief machinist's mate Grove, a methodical man who never mislaid even a dime-store screwdriver, finished fueling the boat. Cotton and Coberth wiped their hands on gobs of waste, nodded, and stepped back. Cotton lit a cigarette. It was safe now to smoke. No one ever smoked while that 100-octane liquid dynamite was being poured into the tanks.

"Wind 'er up," Cotton said.

Machinist's mate Stephens dropped through the engine-room hatch and got the engines going. They were cold. Their song was sour. As they warmed up it became sweeter: a smooth, loud roar with just enough rattle to indicate the tug of unleashed horsepower.

"Good enough," Cotton said, permitting himself a grin.

The starboard engine conked out.

It was the gas. They all knew it, but there was nothing anyone could do about it. The gas was fouled with water which produced bubbles which in turn fouled the engines. When that happened it was not always a simple job to get at the trouble and correct it.

"One of these nights," Stephens prophesied, "we're going to get a dose of this when it'll hurt. Some night out on patrol, with the Japs hot after us."

He wasn't kidding. It was not only possible but probable. The fact that it had not yet happened increased the chance that it was going to. All the boats were in on the risk.

These were dismal nights without that. The Japs had not come down in force since their encounter with Admiral Lee, but for the PT boats the nightly patrols continued. The strain on men's nerves increased as fatigue and sickness sapped their strength. The boys who a few weeks ago had said so glibly, "Gee, look, I lost ten pounds!" were now silent. They had lost twenty.

Back of it all was the feeling, seldom admitted in frank discussion but working deep in each man's mind, that Squadron "X" was luckier than it had any right to be. Such luck could not continue indefinitely, not even among well trained men. Some night it would change.

Some night a boat would go out on patrol as usual, and get blown to hell or return with death aboard, or simply disappear. Maybe those water bubbles in the gas, or a jammed gun, or a stuck torpedo that got cocked and went off—it could be almost anything. Sooner or later it was going to happen.

Not much could be done to cure these jitters. Rest would have helped, but with so many men laid low by dengue fever and malaria, those who remained fit for duty were called upon to go out night after night. Reinforcements would have helped, too. Rumor said they were coming, but Squadron "X" still bore the burden. And mail would have helped. Mail from home would have sent morale soaring again. But none was delivered.

In mid-November survivors from the aircraft carrier *Hornet*, which had been sunk in action, arrived at Tulagi and were assigned to the PT unit. They were quickly trained. And they were sorely needed, as were half a dozen torpedo-boat men, all of them officers, sent out from the States. Then in late November part of another PT Squadron —Squadron "R"—arrived to take up part of the burden.

But Squadron "X" was in bad shape. Boats needed overhauling. Men craved rest. Many were homesick.

The men made the most of what they had: movies, poker, and an occasional small party aboard the tender. Some kind fairy had brought in a few bottles of Scotch and a half dozen cases of beer—a wonderful tonic for jaded nerves, even though severely rationed. When that was gone, a palatable substitute was concocted by diluting medicinal alcohol with water and disguising its rub-down taste with lemon powder.

At Tulagi, too, was a New Zealand corvette in command of a big, rotund man named Britson. He weighed nearly three hundred pounds, and when he laughed, which he did very often, every pound of it rippled. On board his ship he maintained a small but well stocked bar.

The PT skippers paid him a visit every now and then, both to sample his wares and to hear Britson play his accordion. It was an old accordion, battered but sweet, and the songs sung by the New Zealander and his 280 pound executive officer had a rich down-under flavor that was vastly entertaining. Skipper Britson had been around.

"He liked to have us over," Nick says, "to hear our stories. But he seldom let us finish them. 'Now, now,' he'd say, whenever we really got wound up, 'when I was down in—' and off he'd go on a yarn of his own.

"We couldn't match those stories of his. They were stupendous. Even chief storekeeper Robert Eugene Golden, to whom the gang back at the base listened with their mouths open, was out of the running when Britson took off."

The day before Thanksgiving, a cargo ship arrived with holiday food for both Guadalcanal and Tulagi, and the PT unit received its share. Turkey in the Solomons! In the beginning the PT men had eaten Marine food. Later the condition of their larder had varied greatly with the coming, or not coming, of supply ships, and for almost a month there had been little to eat except corned beef and canned spiced ham. Now turkey! Home was practically around the corner!

And on Thanksgiving Day morning, morale went up another notch. Every man on the island who could spare the time from his work stood gazing out at the glassy, mill-pond waters of Sealark Channel. They were watching a minor miracle.

Out of her creek-mouth hiding place had crept the *McFarland*, not now a mere destroyer but a symbol of what determined men could accomplish in the face of impossible handicaps. She was no beauty. Her stern was a nightmare creation that might have been conceived in the mind of Rube Goldberg, autumn brown with rust and tailed with a rudder which appeared to consist mainly of telephone poles. (As a matter of fact the *McFarland's* men *had* used telephone poles. Some had been left in Tulagi's jungle by Japs who apparently had planned to occupy the island permanently.)

Lumbering southward through Sealark, the *Mac* ripped a broad blue gash in the otherwise smooth sea. But she was back from the grave, homeward bound in glory. Cheers followed her. Many a prayer went up that she would get where she was going without further disaster.

She did.

Another American warship, the heavy cruiser *Northampton*, was less fortunate. In a naval engagement off Savo Island November 30, she met disaster.

The motor torpedo boats were not on patrol that night. They had been ordered to remain at their base, so that a force of American warships might enter the area to battle a Jap task fleet which had been reported on its way down from Bougainville. In that battle with the Bougainville Express, the *Northampton* was sunk. At one o'clock in the morning the PT men received word of the sinking and were ordered out to look for survivors.

Five of the boats were in service. All five sped out from Tulagi at once. In the lead were Nikoloric and Lieutenant Westholm, commander of Squadron "R," whose boats were out-board in the nest of PTs at the base when the emergency call was received. Tom Kendall, Brent Greene and Hugh Robinson were not far behind.

The scene into which the little mosquito boats raced was grim indeed. Of the cruiser herself there was no trace; she had gone down some time ago. But men were everywhere in the water, paddling aimlessly about in their life-jackets or clinging to bits of wreckage.

Many had drowned. Some of those in the life-belts were dead. Sharks ranged everywhere, attracted by the blood of the injured.

Worst of all were the survivors who had been burned—and they were many. When the PT men began lifting them aboard, up over the sides and sterns of the rescue boats, some were so horribly seared that there seemed no way to take hold of them.

But there was no crying. Those who could talk at all were only bitter at having lost their ship—and proud, too, in a belligerent kind of way, that they had sunk some Japs before their turn came.

LONG WERE THE NIGHTS

"One man," Nick reports, "was treading water in the midst of some floating debris when we came up to him, and there was a long gray shape in the water just in front of him. His shirt had been burned off in the explosion aboard the ship, and this gray shape—it was a shark about seven feet long—was nuzzling his chest. He kept hitting it with his fists to drive it back. But the shark returned time and again to attack him."

One of the PT's crew ran below and came up with a tommy-gun, two of which were carried as part of the boat's equipment. After that the shark did not linger. With bullets biting his gray hide, he swirled from his intended victim and disappeared straight down at top speed.

But the rescuers had arrived only just in time. The man in the water was terribly weak and when lifted out, collapsed on the deck.

"One of us asked him if he wanted some morphine," Nick recalls. "But he shook his head and said no. He said some of the other fellows would need it more than he did.

" 'Hell,' he said, 'I'm all right. Just tired. What time is it?'

"We told him, and he brought up a grin from somewhere —a feeble, crooked kind of grin, but a grin all the same— and said, 'I was blown off the fantail when the torpedoes hit. Must have been knocked out, because I came to in the water with that shark nudging me in the chest and rolling around for a bite at me. Boy, am I glad to see you guys and get rid of that bastard!' "

He had been in the water nearly five hours.

LONG WERE THE NIGHTS

In all, the boat took aboard more than a hundred survivors, as did the Squadron "R" boat. Kendall, Greene and Robinson picked up more. Some were undoubtedly dead, yet none of the PT men was willing to accept the responsibility of deciding which were dead and which were not, and so all were taken, though the dead men occupied space that might have been used for more of the living.

Nothing much could be done for them while the boats milled about on their Samaritan assignments. The PTs were not equipped for this kind of work. Aboard Nick's boat the total medical supplies consisted of four morphine syrettes and a small amount of Scotch. For the men who asked for cigarettes, the boat had half a carton.

"After half an hour," Nick remembers, "there wasn't room on board to move. They were lying in rows on the deck and standing or sitting in a solid jam below. You had to watch your step, or down you'd go in a heap on top of some poor devil who would not thank you for it. And there were still hundreds of men in the water, patiently waiting for Robbie, Brent or Tom to pick them up.

"Westy and I went back in, and on the way I looked for our shark-fighting friend again. He was still sitting there, leaning against one of the torpedo tubes. I handed him a cigarette, the last one there was, and held a light for him, and he said, 'This is a PT boat, isn't it?'

"I said it was.

" 'All my life,' he said, 'I've wanted to ride one of these

bronchos and see what they can do. Hell, open 'er up and let's get goin'!'

"He was a very brave guy, that seaman. But so were they all."

Chapter Ten

"Bill Blake" is not his name. There was no such name on the PT roster.

Bill was twenty years old—a pleasant, good-natured lad who kept his girl's picture in his locker and faithfully wrote letters to his family. His officers had never found him troublesome. In fact, in censoring his letters they had discovered him to be just a bit sentimental.

On the surface, Bill was a rough, ready boy who enjoyed a scrap—a bit wild, perhaps, but never hard to handle. In action he was cool and steady, and his courage was equal to that of any other man on his boat.

But Bill was changing now. He was forgetting how to laugh. His nerves were taut, his hearing was hypersensitive. He had lost his appetite and become moody, irritable, resentful of the good-natured jibes of his companions.

Bill's trouble was complex but common. Like many of the others he had been out too often on patrol. The long, long nights were getting him.

Bill lived on Snob Hill, and like other occupants of that exclusive suburb had surrounded himself with crude comforts and tried to make the best of Tulagi's drawbacks. One day he walked into his tent and found four of the men playing red-dog there.

"How about it, Bill?" one said. "Sit in?"

LONG WERE THE NIGHTS

Bill said no; he was tired. Kicking his shoes off, he stretched out on his cot and closed his eyes. Around his face, even in repose, were little tell-tale lines of strain and tension.

He slept after a while. But the red-dog game grew noisy and a sudden outburst of hilarity disturbed him. Bill sat up and swung his feet to the floor. His jaw jutted.

"For Pete's sake," he snarled, "do you guys have to do that?"

They stared at him. These men were engineers and gunners, ships' cooks and torpedomen—not psychoanalysts. They thought Bill was kidding.

"Well, well," said one. "We're making too much commotion. Mr. Blake in the next apartment is banging on the radiator."

Bill sat rigidly still on his cot, the little tight lines working about his mouth.

"Mr. Blake is perturbed," said another, grinning.

"Maybe that's funny," said Bill.

"Sure it's funny."

"Well, I don't think so. If you guys have to holler like apes, why'n't you go somewhere else and do it?"

They didn't like Bill's tone and began to be annoyed. "Listen," said one, pointedly. "This game was going on long before you strolled in here. If you don't like the noise, go take a walk."

Bill Blake got up. He was pale now and trembling. Ordinarily at the height of such an argument he would have picked up something and thrown it: a shoe, perhaps, or something else of a strictly non-lethal nature. Then he would have dived at someone's legs and begun a free-for-all, and when the rough and tumble ended, the tension would have ended, too.

This time Bill went out. With a wild look in his eyes he went down the hill to the base and bulled about in the warehouse until he found a tommy-gun. With the gun gripped in unsteady hands, he stormed back to Snob Hill.

Luckily someone saw him coming, and the men had time to scatter. When Bill rushed into the tent, he found it empty.

Bill was worse then. To the rest of what was wrong with him were added bitterness and frustration. He stood in the doorway of the tent and screamed at the men to come back. He threatened to shoot them if they did come back. He brandished the tommy-gun and walked along in front of the tents and shacks, daring anyone to come within range.

"I'll shoot the first guy who comes near me!" he shouted.

The men stayed hidden. No one said much, and no one was sore with Bill. It was too bad, that was all. He was a nice kid but the strain had got him—just as it had undermined the mental stability of some of the Marines on Guadalcanal.

You got that way from facing danger and death night after night without reprieve, and then trying to snatch a few hours of miserable rest during the day with the temperature soaring and the insects driving you crazy. You got it from overwork and constant exposure to tropical sickness. This wasn't Bill's fault. It could have happened to any of them.

After a while Bill tired. He stopped pacing back and forth and sat down, and then Charlie Tufts stepped out of hiding at the base of the hill and began walking up to him.

Charlie was the man for that job: cool, patient, unafraid. He was older than Bill and could talk to the boy as a father to a son. Even when Bill snatched up the tommy-gun and scrambled to his feet again, Charlie continued to walk toward him.

"Now listen, son," Charlie said. "Just take it easy and listen a while . . ."

Bill listened, and when Charlie was through talking to him the boy laid down his tommy-gun and put his face in his hands and sobbed a little. A while later he was over it.

His name was not Bill Blake, and the incident of the tommy-gun is not important. Not in itself. But the story behind it—the drama of the slow and terrible disintegration of men's nerves—is very important indeed.

Because there was beginning to be a little of Bill Blake in nearly everyone.

But the patrols continued. Every day at dusk the PT skippers stood by in the squadron office awaiting reports of the day's scouting. No one could foretell the nature of these reports. It might be "No sign of enemy ships" or it might be "Enemy fleet approaching in force."

In any case the PTs slipped out of hiding with the coming of darkness, and then far into the night they roamed the dangerous waters off Guadalcanal, Savo and Tulagi with engines muffled and feelers extended for trouble—small, swift water-bugs on guard against the octopus.

One night two of the boats were on patrol off Kokumbona, Tom Kendall in one, Nick cruising along behind in another. It was a ghostly kind of night, the moon indistinct but casting a peculiar mist of light in which visibility was distorted.

Aboard Kendall's boat, Blackwood and Todd were on lookout watch, straining their eyes to see through the disturbing haze. Tom Kendall stood just above the cockpit, peering through the glasses.

Suddenly Kendall saw something. He jumped down into the cockpit and passed the glasses to Crumpton.

"Take a look," he said nervously. "What is it?"

Crumpton looked. He had excellent eyes. "That," he said quietly, "is a submarine."

"Right," Tom replied. He swung the boat on target course and called an order to Cavanah. "Tell Nick there's a Jap sub dead ahead and we're firing on it!"

Aboard Nick's boat, the men were weary. They looked at their skipper and waited for the word to head for home. Half the crew was on watch; the others were in the crew's quarters under the forward deck, trying to sleep.

Leon Nale said: "Back home, skipper, except maybe on a Saturday night, I'd have been under the sheets two hours ago. Or did you forget what time it was?"

It was not Nick who answered. It was Woodrow Wilson

Cavanah, aboard Kendall's boat. His banshee voice jerked the whole boat to attention.

"Tawm to Niick! Theyuh's a Jap *sub*-marine out heuh! Can you heuh me? Theyuh's a *sub*-marine out heuh! We are firing on it!"

Bernie O'Neill rushed up into the cockpit and snatched a pair of glasses to con the skipper on the target. Nick scowled at Owen Pearle and said: "Is he kidding? He must be!"

"Maybe they're having difficulty with our wake again," replied Pearle dryly.

Up over the radio came Cavanah. "Tawm to Niick! Theyuh's a Jap *sub*-marine . . ."

Nick looked. That strange misty light was deceptive. He looked again. There, moving along about four hundred yards off the starboard bow at a speed of two knots, was an enemy sub.

Nick's boat closed in fast, her crew scurrying to battle stations. While she was closing, Tom Kendall's boat beat her to the punch and fired four torpedoes. Her men heard the sound of a muffled explosion.

With a bullish roar Nick's boat swept in.

Owen Pearle clung to the starboard gun turret, holding the glasses to his eyes and ignoring the spray that hissed up to blind him. He suddenly forgot he was using multiple vision.

"My God, skipper!" he yelled, as the sub loomed big in the lenses. "Are you trying to *ram* this guy?"

But the PT was not that close. She was just close enough for an accurate torpedo shot. A second later three of her four fish were running. One of them was a hit.

Machinist Red Gartin and gunner Willy Williams exchanged grim glances. They were young, rugged boys, newly added to the crew. They owed the Japs something special. Both were survivors of the aircraft carrier *Hornet*.

But Nick's boat was in trouble.

Aboard the mosquito boat a deafening racket had broken loose. Der and Crosson thought the boat had been hit by enemy shellfire (not from the submarine, which had been surprised before it could fire a shot, but from some other enemy ship unseen in the dark). They fell on the smoke generator and loosed a screen of smoke.

Then they saw their mistake. The PT had not been hit. The last of her four torpedoes had jammed in its tube.

It was the worst hot run the PT had ever experienced. The impulse charge had failed; the torpedo was half out of its tube and raining sparks over the deck. Its propellers whirred. The starting mechanism had been flipped and the fish was working.

Crosson and Nale struggled like madmen to clear it while the boat made her turn and fled for safety. A stench of burning oil gagged them. The hiss of escaping air pressure sang a siren song above the clatter of the torpedo's propeller, deafening them.

Laying smoke in a high-speed retirement, the boat roared on its way while Crosson swung his mallet. But this time the mallet treatment did not work. The fish stayed in the tube, lunging like a mad dog with its tail caught. Every time another sea boiled up over the side, the torpedo-vanes turned and that balky tube of TNT was cocked a little more.

What happened then is not in the PT manual of instructions. The skipper grabbed the wheel and spun it hard over and back again. The boat leaped like a running deer, lunging to one side, then the other, shipping seas that shook her from bow to stern.

The skipper did it again and the little craft stood on her tail and danced a jig, while the sea threw bouquets of spray to her. She thrashed about like a hooked fish, until the torpedo flopped out of its tube. Nick blinked his eyes to make sure it was real.

"Judas!" said Bernie O'Neill, gasping.

Nick grinned. They'd been lucky. "But," he says, "it was a damned fool thing to do, emergency or not, and I don't recommend it. It will never be added to the manual."

Meanwhile the two boats were speeding for home, both trailing smoke. Above them swept an SOC plane from Tulagi, on patrol.

Aboard Nick's boat, not much attention had been paid to what was happening elsewhere, and suddenly, while returning to normal after her series of frantic lunges, she cut across the other boat's bow.

It was close. Very close. Tom Kendall, at the wheel of the other boat, turned his craft without a second to spare, and all aboard her were drenched as she was flung skyward by the wake. Out over the radio went the voice of Woodrow Wilson Cavanah. Said he, soulfully: "Whew!"

And then over the radio came another voice—that of the SOC pilot in the misty haze above. "You guys hit that sub!" he yelled elatedly. "You sank the sonofabitch!"

"Jack and I," Bob recalls, "had been raising beards. Some of the others had tried, too, but most of them had given it up when the whiskers began to itch. Gunner's mate Hill White, who rode Tom's boat, had a fine crop of chin-feathers but shaved them off in a hurry when he went over to Tulagi village one day and saw a Jap prisoner with the same kind of adornment.

"Anyway, ours were luxuriant, black as night and full-blown as bee-hives. No one back home would ever have recognized us.

"But we began to suspect after a time that something other than the Searles brothers was residing in those beards of ours, and so on the afternoon of December 7 we decided to shave them off. It was the anniversary of Pearl Harbor and we thought that would be a way to make note of it.

"We felt naked, almost indecent, after we'd done it. And then we began to worry about our luck. With the whiskers gone our luck might change.

"A lot of us were superstitious like that—not at first, of course, but after we had been out there a while. Some of the psychology profs back home would have held up their hands in horror at the things we used to do—little things like habitually smoking a cigar while waiting for the contact reports before patrol, as Stilly always did, or shaking hands and wishing one another luck, as Barnard and Kuharski used to do before going out.

"There was hardly a man among us, enlisted man or officer, who hadn't some small wrinkle for courting the goddess. Nick had his lucky shoes and never went out without them. In fact he still wears them. Les, Robbie, Brent, Tom —we all believed in something or tried very hard to think we did.

"Among the enlisted men, a good example of what I mean was Tom Sawyer, a quartermaster. He was a slight, thin man who enjoyed nothing more than a poker game. Not red-dog or seven-card-Pete or anything crazy like that, but good straight poker. He was smart, too, knew all the percentages and with any kind of luck would have been the squadron's financier. But the cards eluded him. In game after game he didn't see a face card.

"If anyone ever had a right to grouse, Sawyer did. But he always shrugged it off. 'I'm satisfied,' he used to say. 'Unlucky at cards, lucky with the Japs. If my poker luck changed, the other might change, too. You go right on dealing out the deuces. The day I see a couple of aces back to back I'll tear out and dive into one of Doc Perkins' foxholes!'

"That's how we were—conscious all the time that Squadron 'X' was lucky, but that the luck might change.

LONG WERE THE NIGHTS

"The night of the beard-shaving, there were six boats on patrol, four of ours and two from Squadron 'R.' Stilly Taylor and my gang went up into the slot northwest of Cape Esperance and began beating back and forth to intercept the Japs who had been reported on the way down.

"Les Gamble and Jack were east of us, off Esperance, awaiting the word. The Squadron 'R' boats were behind Savo. Whatever way the enemy came in, he was certain to encounter us.

"Well," Bob continues, "we were beating around hunting trouble, when suddenly, as so often happened on those dark nights, an enemy ship loomed up dead ahead of our boat and we were face to face with all the trouble we could handle.

"There was no chance for a torpedo shot. The Jap, a destroyer, was much too close for that and was tearing along at about thirty-five knots. Our cue was to get away from there and lead him down to the striking force, so I turned the boat and piled on speed. Then the Jap began firing his forward batteries, and by the light of his gun-flashes we saw that he was not alone.

"Bockemuehl, who'd become our radioman when Stephenson left, began calling out information to the other boats while Bill Kreiner spotted for him. 'See three of them!' Kreiner sang out. 'Now four! Now five!' And there were more. There was a whole column of enemy destroyers, screening a transport. But we had the speed to stay ahead of the pack on the way in and were playing the game exactly as we had planned it. Everything was fine.

"Then our starboard engine broke down.

"We had a bad few minutes there. That particular engine had given us trouble before, but Lorran Beed and Winter and Leslie had always been able to make it sing again. They swarmed over it now, down there in the fumes and broiling heat of the engine-room, but this time it would not respond. The leading Jap was ranging us and opened fire with everything he had.

"Right there we lost all interest in leading the enemy into a trap. We had done what we could. The other boats now knew the strength of the approaching fleet and where it was, and our next move was to retire. It was almost too late even for that. Shells were falling around us, splashing into the sea not thirty yards away. The entire Jap fleet was bearing down on us.

"We had a mild case of the horrors. When the enemy began shelling us, I ducked," Bob admits, "which is something I hadn't done since the first night out. All of us were that way. Every man in the squadron, not only on our boat but on all of them, was developing nervous tension to an abnormal degree from going out so often on those nightly trouble-hunts.

"Later the men said they were sure something would happen after Jack and I shaved off our beards. But what they meant, really, was that we had been lucky for too long a time. No boat could be on the select list forever—not even our boat, with Nick's shoes treading her deck.

"So with Blackwood and Colten on the guns, trying to put out the searchlights on the foremost destroyer, we zigzagged out of there and made for Savo Island, where we could hope to hide. At fifteen knots—all the boat would do on two fouled engines—we were practically crawling through the enemy's fire.

" 'Make smoke!' I bellowed.

"Just then a PT boat came thundering out of the dark and went by us, tossing up great white curls of ocean. It was Stilly Taylor and his gang, tearing down to get in ahead of the Japs and take part in the attack.

" '*Get that smoke going!*' I howled.

"Our radio was open. Bockemuehl had been sending out the strength and disposition of the enemy. My yell went out over the air, and Stilly heard it, and he thought I was bellowing at him! Being a very considerate guy, he swung over close to us and laid a lovely smoke screen, just as our own smoke streamed out. If we had planned it that way it could not have worked out any better.

"As it was, we got a thorough drubbing, even with the smoke. Most of the Japs went on by, evidently thinking it more important to protect their troop transport than to chase after our crippled PT boat, but the last one in line turned off to give us a going-over.

"For three minutes he poured shells into the smoke and sprayed it with machine-gun bullets. But our luck held, despite the loss of the beards. The Jap did not hit us, and with Stilly standing by to cover us we reached Savo safely."

But the Japs were not yet excused for the night. When they turned in tight formation toward the Guadalcanal shore to cover the landing of troops from their transport, the PT striking force darted in to attack.

To the Japs it came as a complete surprise. They had apparently thought themselves insured now against further molestation. Before they could assemble their wits they were suddenly under assault from four directions.

It was a swift, savage attack, a five-minute drama made up of countless smaller ones. The transport was the PTs' target for the night. The four flying thunder boats stung their way in the dark through the enemy's shield of destroyers to place their barbs in the big ship's vitals. Enemy troops jammed her decks, milling about in panic as the thunderbolts slashed at her from what must have seemed a score of directions.

Jap shells criss-crossed the dark. Tracers and searchlights cut the night into a pattern of livid rectangles. But for the Japs there were too many PTs and the little boats struck too swiftly.

Jack Searles picked a course through the curtain of fire which took his boat to within fifty feet of an enemy destroyer. Searchlights blinded him and shells missed him by whispers. But he went on in. Weaving and dodging, he drove at the transport and sent two fish flying. He hit it.

The Squadron "R" skippers hurled their boats at the troopship but were trapped. They turned their torpedoes on the destroyers, hit two of them and ran.

Les Gamble, the Frisco Kid, sent his boat flying between

two of the screening destroyers and closed the transport. Beside him, spotting, stood his new exec, Sidney Rabekoff (Lieutenant jg of New York City) who possessed a really remarkable pair of eyes and could out-see a cat in the dark. Big Clarence Schrock, the quartermaster, grinned cheerfully and urged the skipper on.

"Come on, skipper!" Schrock said. "Let's get in there! Let's throw 'em a bowline!"

They were a good crew. Their score proved it. And whatever Les Gamble elected to do with the hurtling little thunder boat beneath them was all right with every man aboard. Down in the engine-room, old-timer Harlan Gilgore and Clifton Johnson calmly worked at their jobs while the boat roared in—Johnson quietly chewing the cold butt of a huge black stogie. Ready at the tubes was torpedoman Lott, a quiet, religious man who said little but knew every wrinkle of his job.

At three hundred yards Gamble fired two torpedoes, then turned to retire. He saw then what he thought was another transport off shore, and loosed his remaining two torpedoes. The second "transport" was a beached hulk, relic of an earlier Jap attempt to storm the island. It burst into flames.

So did the first one.

Then the mosquito fleet sped out again, unscathed. Their speed and the audacity of their attack had carried them safely through the enemy's frantic attempts to halt them. The damage was done before the confused Japs could bring into action the full power of their heavier guns.

Behind, as the PTs sped for home, lay a scene to inspire Doré. Off Lunga Point an enemy destroyer was sinking, his fantail down, flames hungering fiercely at his bow. Not far away a second destroyer had erupted in flames, and from the heart of the inferno a column of black smoke soared upward to blend with the darkness.

Off shore the troopship, hit by at least two torpedoes and possibly more, lowered her nose and exploded, and the sound was a deep-throated roar that walked on giant feet along the peaks of the neighboring islands, smothering the cries of the enemy troops in the water. Again she blew up. Again the sound rolled out through the night and flames burst from her innards.

Four times the troopship was rocked and the night rocked with her. Then beneath a painted sky she rolled on her side and sank, showing her stern in the boiling sea for an instant before she vanished. After her, sucked under by her plunge, went scores of the little struggling shapes who had leaped but a moment before from her fiery decks.

The enemy had had enough. Less than an hour before, eight to ten destroyers and a troop-crowded transport had boldly steamed into Sleepless Lagoon. Now the remaining ships fled northward, leaving a littered sea and a smoking sky behind them.

Two destroyers and the troopship—and countless enemy troops—failed to make the return trip to Bougainville.

Chapter Eleven

NICK was on Guadalcanal one day, on an errand for Robbie, when some prisoners were brought in. The captured Japs were a sorry lot, their ill-fitting clothes smeared with blood and mud and hanging in rags. Most were fearful and surly. One, however, eagerly advanced on the staring Marines and waved a hand glibly in greeting.

"Hiya, fellers," he said in perfect English. "Anybody here from Frisco?"

He seemed disappointed when no one responded.

"A number of the Japs spoke fairly good English," Bob reports, "and some were really expert. For instance: the radiomen on the Bougainville Express often put out feelers to the PT boats, hoping we would fall for the trick and give away our position.

"You'd hear a cultured voice come up on the radio with something like, 'Can you receive me? Are you getting me okay?' and if you happened to be doing some day-dreaming at the time, you just might be dumb enough to answer."

The Japs were beginning to be discouraged monkeys, too. On Guadalcanal their troops were encountering difficulties in their campaign to push the Americans into the sea. All attempts to retake the airfield had been frustrated, and Jap

LONG WERE THE NIGHTS

strength on the island was waning. Their navy continued to struggle to bring in new men.

The Jap admirals were apparently not yet ready to launch another armada such as the one sunk in the Battle of Guadalcanal, but in the early part of December they stabbed repeatedly and persistently with small, speedy forces.

On one of those nights Jack Searles and a boat from Squadron "R" were on patrol together off the Guadalcanal shore. The night was dark. The Japs were up to something and the PTs knew it. Officers and men were doubly alert as she prowled the waters with her engines muffled.

Suddenly against the darker shadows of the shore an enemy submarine surfaced. Up it came like a black ghost from the sea's depths, to sit silently on the water. Out from the beach sped a Jap landing barge, to meet the sub and discharge passengers.

Obviously these were important passengers.

Jack's boat moved in, but her approach posed a problem. The Squadron "R" boat was too close to the sub to fire her torpedoes and was squarely in the line of fire of Jack's boat.

But there was not time for further maneuvering. At any moment the enemy might discover his danger and crash-dive to safety.

Jack and Al Snowball (Lieutenant Alfred A. Snowball of Niles, Ohio), the new executive officer, held a whispered conference and quietly sent out the call to general quarters. On target course the boat stealthily slipped forward. Suddenly two torpedoes sped from her tubes.

It was a close call. One of the fish, speeding toward its target, passed directly underneath the stern of the Squadron "R" boat. But both torpedoes found the mark. On the submarine's side, two dull red glows suddenly appeared.

Then an explosion shook the night. The sub shuddered, broke in half, and sank.

The Squadron "R" boat, quick now to act, raced toward the Jap landing barge which had almost reached the beach. Roaring down on it, the PT opened fire with her machineguns, strafed her victim thoroughly, then drew alongside.

She had done a good job. She took the barge in tow and an hour later was back at the base with her prize.

Jack Searles was awarded the Navy Cross for his work that night. It had been a difficult assignment, executed with skill and daring. Like Lieutenant Hugh Robinson, now in command of the squadron, the older Searles brother possessed the gift of leadership and had proved time and again his wizardry in the use of the PTs' most formidable weapon —the element of surprise. Quiet and slightly grim, he worked out his plans of attack with the utmost care, and they were seldom unsuccessful. His list of achievements was second only to that of Les Gamble, the squadron's high scorer.

To Lieutenant Al Snowball and the eight enlisted men of the crew, the navy awarded the Silver Star for "participation in a daring operation which thwarted an important enemy mission."

LONG WERE THE NIGHTS

This was not the original crew.[1] Of those, only three now remained. The others were ill or had been transferred to other boats in an effort to keep as many craft in commission as possible. Squadron "X" was no longer observing the formalities.

Two nights later, tragedy struck at the PT fleet.

Perhaps it was overdue. Perhaps in their ceaseless nocturnal sorties against superior enemy forces, the little motor torpedo boats had indeed been luckier—as some of the men soberly believed—than they had any right to be.

Night after night they had hit the enemy hard and then fled back to their base, leaving Jap ships in distress behind them: burning, sinking ships on which men were being hurt and killed. Yet their own losses had been incredibly small.

Joe Nemec had died, but the Japs had not done that. Nor could the enemy be held responsible for the fact that nearly every man in the PT fleet had suffered or was suffering from malaria, dengue fever, or nervous exhaustion. The fact remained that no PT had been sunk. None had even been permanently put out of action.

---

[1] The enlisted men who received the Silver Star were:
Harold C. Johnson, quartermaster 1st class
George W. Ebersberger, Jr., machinist's mate 1st class
Thomas S. MacMillan, radioman 2nd class
Harold C. Crouch, machinist's mate 2nd class
Cletus E. Osborne, gunner's mate 2nd class
Stephen Yando, machinist's mate 1st class
Emil P. Stayonovich, torpedoman 2nd class
Charles A. Pellinat, seaman 1st class

LONG WERE THE NIGHTS

This night their luck changed. The enemy came in force, determined still to bolster the strength of his troops on beleaguered Guadalcanal. Reconnaissance reports indicated a force of destroyers and some transports, and possibly a Japanese submarine. The Japs were expected to attempt a landing.

The PT fleet deployed to meet the enemy with a triple-barbed attack. The boat captained by Stilly Taylor beat back and forth on patrol between Tassafaronga and Doma Reef with a Squadron "R" boat. The striking force, waiting south of Savo Island, included a PT skippered by Les Gamble, another in command of Jack Searles, and Bob's boat, in charge of exec Bill Kreiner. Bob Searles had gone on an errand to Guadalcanal and had not returned.

A pair of Squadron "R" boats moved quietly up the line to hunt the reported enemy submarine. One of them had the ill luck to find an uncharted reef instead, and went aground. The other continued on her mission, failed to find any submarine, and returned to help her sister boat.

It was growing late. Eleven o'clock came. On his boat, Jack Searles listened with increasing anxiety to the radioed reports of the progress—or lack of progress—being made in getting the stricken PT off the reef, and with the Japs due in, he decided to do what he could to help. His boat left the other two boats of the striking force and sped through the night on her rescue mission.

At half past twelve, one of Tulagi's SOC biplanes, the eyes of the PT fleet, spotted the enemy force moving down through the slot, and radioed the warning.

"Enemy destroyers," came the report, growling ominously from the speakers mounted on the PTs' cockpits. "Six, seven, eight—at least nine of them. Other enemy ships not identified . . ."

South of Savo Island, the two remaining boats of the striking force prepared swiftly for action. The gunners crawled into their turrets. Torpedomen stood by the tubes. With Les Gamble and Bill Kreiner at the wheels, the boats moved in, met the advancing Jap force and attacked.

Gamble went in first. An enemy destroyer loomed in the dark ahead, and the PT, on collision course, fired her four torpedoes. At least one of them was an unquestioned hit. The enemy ship burst into flames.

The other boat, Kreiner at the wheel and Meadows conning her in, took the second Jap in line and loosed her spread of torpedoes. A red glow colored the destroyer's stern, like blood seeping slowly from ruptured flesh.

The two boats turned to retire and were spotted. Jap searchlights leaped out to snare them. With smoke pouring out astern, the PTs raced side by side through enemy fire, made good their escape, and headed for Tulagi. Behind them their combining trails of smoke formed a strange white wall which reached in an almost unbroken line from Cape Esperance to Savo.

Out over the air from the fleeing boats' radiomen had gone that now familiar call for assistance: "Hurry, hurry! William is on our tail!" Of those who heard it, Stilly Taylor was nearest and moved up to intercept the pursuing Jap.

Stilly ran up at full speed through the dark. Beside him ship's cook Henry Bracy, who had the eyes of a cat, searched the night through glasses. Suddenly Bracy turned.

"Smoke ahead, skipper," he said. "And a Jap 'can,' I think."

They had run on that long white wall of smoke left by the two fleeing boats. Like a barrier it stretched across before them, extending left to right. At its left end an enemy destroyer was bulling in.

The Jap reached the barrier and stopped, apparently unwilling to plunge into the smoke. He circled slowly, scarcely moving, frustrated and irresolute. Stilly fingered the PT's throttles and eased the mosquito boat to a silent crawl.

"He's hardly moving," Bracy reported. "He don't seem to know what to do next, skipper."

The PT sneaked into position. Her torpedoes went winging, and suddenly the night shuddered. Up from the sea where the Jap had been sitting rose a hurtling tower of water which to the watching men on the PT boat seemed as high as the peaks on Savo Island. Up and up it went, a great white chunk of ocean flung skyward by the exploding Jap.

With her tubes empty, her engines wide open, the PT bellowed a roar of triumph and headed for the barn. Les Gamble and Bill Kreiner and their crews were there when she arrived. Out in Sleepless Lagoon, the PTs' smoke screen still hovered over the grave of the shattered Jap destroyer, while another Jap, hit by either Gamble or Kreiner or both, blazed redly like a giant flare in the dark.

The PT skippers and their men stood around at the base, awaiting the arrival of the rest of the fleet. They were in good spirits. They had done a good job. Some of them went aboard Tom Kendall's boat, which had not been assigned to patrol that night, and passed the time pleasantly by listening to canned music. Tom and his crew had chipped in to buy an electric phonograph and some records from departing Marines. After a sortie with the Japs, it was pleasant to relax and listen to dance music. It was good for the nerves.

But suddenly up over the radio came Jack Searles' voice. Jack had been out there in the thick of things, "tearing around and getting fired on by damn' near the whole Jap fleet." Now, flatly, his voice delivered bad news.

"We have just picked up a fireman off Frank Freeland's boat," he said. "There may be other survivors out here. Better come out and look around."

It was almost dawn, about four-thirty o'clock. Les Gamble went aboard Stilly's boat and, the phonograph behind them now silent, the PT went out on its grim mission. Between Savo Island and the area in which the Jap destroyer had blown from the water, they found Jack's boat beating back and forth at slow speed. Scattered over the sea was the wreckage of a Squadron "R" boat which had been skippered by Lieutenant Frank Freeland.

There was no longer any pressure from the enemy. Battered and disorganized, he had fled. Now in the dim light of dawn, the two PTs painfully scoured the sea for survivors. They found three bodies.

Abandoning her search, Stilly's boat turned toward Savo Island, where it was at least possible that some of the missing men might have reached safety by swimming.

Dawn was breaking then. The sea ran white against the little island's rugged shoreline, forming a soft pearl necklace at the throat of her shadowed peaks. Water birds flashed in the light, shrilling above the boat. Among the rocks lay patches of yellow oil from the sunken Japs.

There at the water's edge something moved, and the men on the PT sent up a shout. The shout was answered. The mosquito boat nosed inshore, warily feeling her way through treacherous shoals until it was not safe to go closer; then she launched a rubber boat and two men rowed to the beach. Back with them they brought Lieutenant (jg) Charlie Melhorn, who had been riding the Squadron "R" boat that night.

He told them what had happened.

The Squadron "R" boat had been one of the pair which went sub-hunting early in the evening. With her sister boat aground on the reef, she had hovered near, trying to help, until called back to join the striking force. On her way back she encountered the incoming Jap force and was chased out of the area.

She circled, moved in again. The Japs were still searching for her with their shells at long range. Suddenly one of the shells screeched over the mosquito boat's windshield, crashed through her plywood deck as through a taut sheet of paper, and burst with a deafening detonation in the hot, crowded confines of her engine-room.

It was a death blow. The fragile torpedo boats are nowhere protected by armor, and any hit aft of the bridge is almost certainly fatal. Flames leaped through the splintered deck and spread hungrily forward, devouring all that they touched. The sea poured in through the little boat's wounds. From the inferno in her engine-room came cries of men in pain, loud against the sudden terrible silence of her demolished engines.

For a moment, still making some headway, the PT circled crazily through the enemy's fire, while those who were still alive on her blasted deck struggled dazedly to their feet. One of the first to find himself was her skipper, Frank Freeland.

He tried to reach the engine-room and was hurled back by the flames. Stumbling forward, he shouted orders. The men rallied to the sound of his voice.

There was not much time. Every man aboard the boat knew that. She was mortally hit, the flames consuming what remained of her with a vast, noisy hunger. At any second they would reach her gas-line or the three thousand gallons of aviation gas in her tanks.

But her men were brave. When the order was given to abandon ship, they worked desperately to get a rubber boat inflated and put it overside. The PT, now without headway, rolled drunkenly in the sea and reddened the night with her raging fires.

The rubber boat splashed over. The first of the men fell sprawling into it, picked himself up and reached for the next. Two others—Fireman Darling and Charlie Melhorn—found themselves cut off by the smoke and heat and dived into the sea.

Then the fiery hell in the PT's engine-room reached her gasoline tanks and she exploded like a pricked balloon. The rubber boat at her side went with her. Nothing was left.

Aboard the rescue boat, Melhorn shook his head slowly and looked out at the dawn-lit stretch of sea where it had happened. "We had to jump," he said. "Darling and I, we had to jump. We couldn't reach the others to help with the rubber boat. A second later the boat exploded. All at once—like that—one tremendous explosion. I was slammed through the water and passed out, and when I came to I was swimming. There was a Jap ship burning off the Guadalcanal shore—one of you boys had torpedoed it—and I got my bearings and just kept on swimming in what I hoped was the direction of Savo—and made it." He rubbed his eyes, as though seeing the ghosts of his shipmates out there. "Oh God," he said softly. "Oh my God, those guys. They never had a chance."

Chapter Twelve

THE new enrollee in the Hard Rock Club—the Squadron "R" boat which had gone aground—had spent the night on the reef where she was stuck fast. Next morning Hugh Robinson and another boat went out to get her off.

Their trip was productive in more ways than one. In Sleepless Lagoon they came upon an abandoned Jap gig— an officers' motor launch—drifting aimlessly with the tide. Machinist's mate Oliver Shaw and ship's cook Joe Koval boarded the tiny craft and discovered to their great delight that its inboard motor was in working order. They promptly christened it the *Stinky Maru* and ran it back to Tulagi. They were the right men for that job. Both had grown bristling mustachios and looked like pirates in an old-style melodrama.

The PTs continued on their way. Presently they were nosing through the wreckage of the enemy destroyer sunk by Stilly Taylor the night before. Dapper Joe Kernell, a skipper now that Robbie had been appointed squadron commander, took his pipe from his mouth, rubbed the thread of mustache which he fondly believed was the image of Clark Gable's, and suddenly touched Robbie's arm.

"Look," he said. "For Pete's sake—Japs!"

There were three of them, clinging to a piece of wreckage. The PT swung toward them and Robbie went forward.

With a forty-five in his hand he motioned the three hapless Japs to come aboard.

They were reluctant, but two at length swam to the boat and were hauled in by the PT's crew. The last of the trio clung stubbornly to his bit of debris, refusing to follow their ignoble example. Made of sterner stuff, he apparently preferred death by drowning to the humility of capture.

Robbie talked to him and brandished the pistol. The Jap shook his head, refusing even to answer. Then one of the PT's crew stepped to Robbie's side with a thirty-caliber rifle and drew a bead on the Jap's head.

The Jap changed his mind. He swam to the boat and joined his companions huddled on deck. The three of them —all petty officers—crouched there shivering with cold and fear and watching every move of the PT's crew.

They were determined little men. To the questions fired at them by Robbie and Joe Kernell they replied in chattering Japanese, employing just enough English to insist that they knew none at all. When it penetrated their terror that they were not to be killed, their attitude changed and they became surly. But still they spoke no English.

"Christmas Eve," Bob recalls, "was both gay and tragic. For those of us who were not scheduled to go out on patrol, it was a fairly pleasant evening. For those who did go out, it was an interlude they would like to forget.

"We had looked forward to Christmas and arranged a little shindig aboard the tender. Some of us had some

liquor—not much, but a little of this and a little of that—
and brought it out. But then after a long and serious discussion we decided not to use it. We owed ourselves a bit of a binge on New Year's Eve, we argued, and there wasn't enough of the wherewithal for both nights. So the little of this and the little of that were put away again, not without some groans, and we substituted a bottle of medicinal alcohol.

"Mixing that stuff to make it palatable was something of an art, accomplished through the use of powdered fruit juices—lemon and orange, principally. It made a potent punch, thanks to the testing and tasting of Bill Kreiner, who did most of the blending. Then we sat around, each man with his minute share, and opened up a bag of mail which had just come in.

"It was a wonderful feeling to have mail from home at Christmas time, when you were a world apart from all the folks you wanted so much to see. A very wonderful feeling. And one of the letters was from Commander Montgomery, saying he felt better and was going to make out all right. That was good news to all of us. The commander was one of the finest men we had ever known, understanding as hell about everything, and just knowing that he was on the mend was as nice a Christmas present as we could ask.

"So there in the PT officers' quarters on the tender, with Skipper Beasley watching over us, we did our best to capture the Christmas spirit with mail, a couple of drinks, a guitar and some songs. The songs were mostly Hawaiian, sung by Lieutenant Clark Faulkner, commander of some Squadron 'T' boats which had just come in. No one felt like singing Christmas carols—or anyway, no one sang any.

"Meanwhile, some of the other boys were out on patrol."

Tom Kendall's boat was one of those on patrol that Christmas Eve, but there was little to arouse in her crew the spirit of Christmas. They had been assigned that night to a new patrol extension southwest of Guadalcanal. No one knew much about this area, and existing charts of it were inaccurate.

The moon was bright. Every rock, every smallest object protruding from the sea, cast a shadow. The crew kept "seeing things" because of these shadows. All were nervously on edge and glumly wondering how the parties ashore were progressing without them. They envied, with reason, those who had been lucky enough to escape patrol duties this night.

Suddenly Kendall, searching the sea through glasses, saw what appeared to be a ship. He studied it for a moment. It seemed to be moving, but the light was so deceptive and the sea there so choked with reefs that the motion might be an illusion. Tom passed the glasses to Crumpton, the quartermaster, who was the boat's exec in everything but name.

"What is it?" Tom asked.

"It looks to me like a Jap destroyer, skipper."

"Tell Cavanah to send out the word we've spotted an enemy ship. Ask if there's a plane up to come over and look at it, and see if there are any others around."

Crumpton relayed the order, and Cavanah sent it out. Meanwhile a Squadron "R" boat had come up. Her men, too, looked the Jap over and prepared for action. Both boats then lay quiet, impatiently waiting for an answer to the request for aerial observation.

The plane did not come. The moon remained bright, and aboard the PT Kendall and his crew grew uneasy. At any moment the Jap might spot them.

"All right," Kendall said at last, "let's move in. Tell the 'Ron 'R' boat we're attacking."

The PT advanced warily, feeling for position, while Crumpton lined up the target. She had a veteran crew, this boat. Every man aboard her had seen his full share of action, and so well did they know their jobs that Kendall seldom had to issue an order. Efficiently they moved in to attack, while the Squadron "R" boat deployed to starboard.

Both boats fired four torpedoes. The enemy ship was a perfect target. But the Jap did not move.

Said Crumpton, peering in bewilderment through the glasses: "Something tells me, skipper, we've made a mistake."

The PT cautiously moved in closer. Crumpton was right. Their "Jap" was a rock which nature had fashioned in the shape of a ship. The strange, shadowy moonlight and the movement of the water there on a submerged reef had completed the illusion. The two PTs turned about and headed for home.

On the way, a little while later, they passed two other torpedo boats moving down into the area they had just left. And then, in answer to Kendall's radioed call for air support, two planes from Guadalcanal appeared in the sky above.

What happened then was "one of those things"—excusable because all pilots must at one time be green, and because communications in the Guadalcanal area were often fouled by atmospheric conditions beyond any man's control.

Spotting the two motor torpedo boats moving down toward "Kendall's Rock," the planes mistook them for enemy ships. They, too, may have been confused by the strange brilliance of the moon that night. In any case, the foremost plane peeled off, swooped down over the mosquito boats, and loosed its load of bombs. All about the startled PTs the sea was smashed upward in fountains of spray.

For an instant the officers and men on the trapped boats were too astonished to act. Then, doubling their speed, the little boats frantically began zigzagging in an effort to escape, while their radiomen screamed at the planes to break off the attack. Boats and planes were on the same radio frequency. The pilots should have heard.

Evidently they did not. Ominously the second plane swept in for the kill, her bombs poised. In self-defense the PT gunners were forced to open fire. With all guns blazing, the two boats desperately ran for home.

They were not hit. Their curtain of fire kept the planes

at a distance until at last the screams of the radiomen reached the erring pilots' ears. But some damage had been done. Calling the base on the way in, the skipper of one boat said glumly: "We have a wounded man aboard—shrapnel wound. Please ask the doctor to be at the dock."

And his next remark came over the radio, too, though perhaps it was not meant to. In a low, bitter voice he added: "What a lousy Christmas present we got."

But occasionally the PT skippers made mistakes, too. Mistakes were natural in that area of constant upheaval where the South Pacific war was being waged under conditions which bred everlasting confusion. High-scoring Les Gamble, as cool a man as the squadron could boast, made a mistake for which he paid a most entertaining price.

Gamble was on routine patrol that night, beating back and forth in the dark. The weather was bad. There was little wind, and the sea was calm enough, but muggy, low-lying rain clouds had squeezed the night into a shallow concentration of darkness. Gamble and Sid Rabekoff, his exec, kept their eyes open for trouble.

It had been a difficult patrol from the start. Radio communications were jumbled and the disposition of the PT boats was uncertain. All at once the men on the PT saw a ship. No friendly vessels had been reported in the vicinity. This one, therefore, was a Jap.

The Gamble technique was working nicely. With exquisite stealth the PT made her approach, caught the shadowed outline of the enemy ship in her sights, and loosed two torpedoes.

The two fish straddled the ship, one skimming past her bow, the other barely clearing her stern. It was probably the only time Les Gamble ever missed so tempting a target.

"Damn!" he said.

Then up over the radio came a voice—the deep, chesty voice of Britson, New Zealand skipper of a corvette. Said Britson, with indignation in every lordly syllable:

"Are you intrepid little bawstards trying to sink *me?*"

Gamble swallowed hard and looked at Rabekoff and Schrock. They all took another long look at the "Jap." Gamble stepped unsteadily to the radio and stood there beside the radioman, moistening his lips. Lester Gamble, despite his impressive record, was by nature a shy and retiring individual.

"Y-yes, sir," he finally managed. "I guess we were."

"I thought so," replied Britson in a voice of darkest severity containing just the hint of a chuckle. "I certainly thought so. By the lord, the bar of this ship will be closed henceforth and forever to all PT men!" There was a pause—and then a sound which was a chuckle beyond any doubt. "I'll expect an explanation as soon as you report back in."

It was a red-faced Gamble who went aboard the corvette an hour or so later. Even the presence of Tom Kendall, whom he had brought along for something on which to lean, was no great comfort. Skipper Britson, all three hundred pounds of him, stood waiting with legs spread wide, hands on his hips, in the captain's cabin.

Britson's eyes twinkled. His scowl was aquiver at the corners. "Mister Gamble," he said, "sit down."

Les sat.

"What, Mister Gamble, would you like to drink?"

Les looked at him warily. "Why—uh—anything."

"Good," said Britson. "Because I have a drink for you, Mister Gamble. A very special drink—especially for you." He produced a pewter mug in which numerous ingredients, including gin, rum, beer and whiskey, had been blended. It was a mixture to make any man reluctant.

Les looked at it, raised it timidly to his lips and looked again at the corvette's skipper. He drank it.

"All," said Britson with a full moon of smile, "is forgiven." He sat down and chuckled. Every pound of him rippled with mirth.

With nothing more sinister in the offing than a hangover, the high-scoring ace of Squadron "X" heaved a sigh of relief and staggered to his bed.

Chapter Thirteen

ROUTINE at Sesapi was by now fairly well established. If lucky enough to have alternate nights off, the officers usually rose about seven in the morning on their patrol days, had breakfast aboard the tender and then went to the base to check the servicing of the boats. What remained of the morning was spent in censoring the outgoing mail, attending their own personal needs, and going over plans for the coming night's operations.

After lunch on the tender, they played cards, slept, or simply killed time until the patrols were due to go out. Then began the tension.

"You began to feel it," says Bob, "while waiting in the operations office for the radio reports. No one did any clowning then. We were always very quiet, and you could feel your nerves getting tight and the sweat coming out on you."

They all felt it. And when the officers went down to the boats, the enlisted men would be there waiting—very quietly waiting—for news of what might be in store for them. Some would say with studied indifference, "What's the dope on tonight, skipper?" as though it didn't matter.

It mattered. The lines of strain on the men's faces—faces grown old and tired—said quite plainly that it mattered. One night an unthinking man who did not have to go out on patrol remarked carelessly that a big enemy force was on the way. His buddies asked their officers if it were true, and learned that it was not. They blacklisted the rumor-spreader for days.

But Japs or not, the patrols went out and usually it was dawn when they returned. Then those who had ridden the boats had breakfast and if the heat was endurable, slept off some of the tension and fatigue.

The enlisted men followed much the same routine as the officers. But the men were jealous of their boats and made frequent trips to the base, even when not needed, to supervise the work being done there.

"At times it was difficult," Nick says, "to get them to turn things over to the base force. They were touchy about the equipment on their boats and had to be sure that nothing was done without their approval. They were the ones who had to work with these things in times of danger, and if anyone monkeyed with the boats without their knowledge, it was just too bad. Some of them would have worked twenty-four hours a day if not forced to rest."

They were a motley crew, officers and men alike. Formalities in the matter of wearing apparel had been abandoned some time ago. Clothes were issued without cost in combat areas, and the men took what was given them and wore it or not, as the mood suited.

The most popular garb consisted of shoes and shorts. Some wore shirts in the faint hope that the mosquitoes might thereby be discouraged. Others wore Marine fatigue clothes.

LONG WERE THE NIGHTS

Anything was acceptable. At night, on patrol, they usually wore flying suits, life-jackets and helmets.

Most of the men were Snob Hillers by now. The officers were less fortunate. Accommodations for them aboard the tender were far from luxurious. The supply of bunks was limited, and Tulagi's assorted insects had acquired a fancy to the ship and moved in to take up permanent residence, despite determined efforts to keep them out.

But at least the tender was dry. Snob Hill was not. The constant rains had made a deep brown soup of the suburb's "streets" and the Seat of Meditation stood usually in a foot of water.

"You need a pilot," said Crosson, "to get in and out of here."

"Even the birds," said Woodrow Wilson Cavanah, "don't come here any more. There's no place for 'em to light."

Said Der: "You roll over in your sleep and you're like to strangle in the mud. You drop a card out of your sleeve playing poker, and you need a dredge to get it back."

There were mosquitoes, too, to offset the advantages of space and fresh air. Even those men fortunate enough to have obtained collapsible tropic-weather huts with walls of screening were annoyed by the pests.

Moreover, Snob Hill was no longer exclusive. With part of Squadron "R" now based at Sesapi and part of Squadron "T" moving in, conditions were fast becoming crowded. But at heart the Snob Hillers were proud of their self-made suburb. When some of the officers elected to quit the tender's crowded quarters and seek more spacious accommodations elsewhere, few of the men chose to accompany them.

Robbie, Les Gamble, Tom Kendall and some of the others had been exploring, and down the shore from Sesapi a mile or so they had located an interesting little river—not really a river, but a clear, wide-mouthed stream that chuckled intriguingly out of a tangle of green jungle. Where this stream, the Maliali, ran crystal clear into Tulagi harbor stood a native village. The boys inquired around, talked to the occupants of the place, and discovered that it could be rented. They rented it.

Maliali was a pleasant change from the crowded tender. Back from the tangled vegetation at the river's edge stretched a broad brown clearing dotted with native huts which, though shaggy with overhanging thatch, appeared to be habitable. Feather-duster palms rustled a friendly welcome. The mud, though present, was no great drawback. There was even a church.

"That church," said Al Snowball, speculatively eyeing it, "would make a first class place to show Commander Beasley's movies."

Others agreed with him. The church was big; its grass roof was thick and its walls were elaborately designed. At night it should be cool enough to provide all the comforts of an air-conditioned theater on Broadway.

The base force went to work on it, rigged up a generator for electric power and installed the tender's moving-picture projector. Spirits were high. The men picked out their new homes, flipped coins to decide priority, and set up their cots. Those who had bunked on the tender brought over their mattresses. Pictures of wives and sweethearts went up quickly, and before long a phonograph was pouring out cheerful music.

New Year's Eve was a night to remember. Patrol tension was forgotten for a time when some of the PT men gathered in the C.P.O. mess aboard the tender. From the wardroom they pilfered a silver pitcher, and with it, on the table, they placed a slab of ice in a washbowl.

The men had been saving their "little of this" and "little of that" for the occasion. Now, with Bill Kreiner standing by as bartender, each man filed past the washbowl and poured his contribution into it. It was not much, even when assembled, but the resulting New Year's punch was at least an amazing blend of surprises.

Kreiner tasted it and wrinkled up his nose. "Lousy," was his verdict. "What this needs is some of those powdered fruit juices." He obtained some and opened them with great ceremony. He also found some sugar and some medicinal alcohol, then added some pineapple juice and sampled the mixture again. "Better," he decided.

He added some of the medicinal alcohol and some lemon juice. "Still better. Brent, you taste it. Isn't that better?"

"It would never go in Louisville," said Brent, shaking his head.

Tom Kendall stepped up, tried it, shut his eyes with a grimace. "Or in Minneapolis," he said. "We used to drink stuff like that at Northwestern, but I'm older now and more careful."

"You fellows just don't appreciate good bartending," Bill complained.

He stirred in another soupçon of sugar and held a glassful of the mixture to the light—a proud dowager examining the color and texture of vintage wine. "Jake, you try it."

"Don't give him any," said Nick. "He high-hatted us. He wouldn't move to Maliali."

Jake Kearney stepped up, grinning, and sampled the punch. "All it needs," he said, "is some good advertising and we could make a fortune on it. 'Tulagi Torpedo Cocktail.' That's it. Boy, we're in." Jake had been in the advertising business back home.

Joe Kernell tasted the stuff and quickly sat down, fingering his Clark Gable mustache to be sure it had not been scorched. "My, my," he said.

"Is that approval or criticism?" Kreiner demanded.

"My, my," Joe repeated.

Kreiner returned to his punch bowl and injected a few more ingredients. Sidney Rabekoff screwed up his courage and assayed it.

"Two of those," Sidney declared, "and I could fly home to the Bronx, like that fellow in a story I heard once." He told the story. Sidney's dialect stories were unforgettable.

"Try one on The Ace," suggested Les Gamble. "He'll

take it for a touchdown."

Al Snowball grinned and accepted the challenge. He was big and rugged, and had played football at Amherst. But the Tulagi Torpedo was too much even for him, and he fumbled.

"If the colonel had one of these," said Al, "maybe he'd believe me."

They laughed a long time at that one. Over on Guadalcanal one day, Al had encountered a certain Marine colonel. "My name," the colonel said, "is Blizzard." Al looked at him, gulped, backed quickly to the nearest exit and said with the straightest face he could manage: "Mine, sir, is Snowball—and I can prove it."

It was Jim Mountcastle's turn. He tasted the mixture and smiled. "Very good," he said. "You know, this whole place agrees with me, somehow. I was underweight when I got here. Had asthma, too, sort of. But since I landed on Tulagi I've felt like a million dollars."

"These Virginia guys," said Stilly. "You can't keep 'em down. But hell, look at Kreiner. And Brent. Ever since they got here they've been getting healthier while the rest of us went down hill like a landslide. What do you weigh now, Bill? Four hundred?"

"A mere two-ten," Kreiner sighed. "But I have hopes. Maybe if I settled down in this part of the world I wouldn't be so puny." He put the last of the alcohol into the punch and passed a glass to Doc Lastreto. "Analyze this, Doc. You're always craving action."

Lastreto tried it. He was a short, barrel-chested man with a Groucho Marx mustache—a lieutenant, junior grade, from San Francisco. The fact that he was the squadron doctor sometimes disturbed him. It had caused Robbie to insist that he stay off the boats, on which Doc had been riding at every opportunity in a fervent desire to encounter some Japs.

"It should be labeled 'Poison'," Doc pronounced. "But fortunately there isn't enough to poison very many of us."

Kreiner served the drinks. Tom Kendall made up a song about the paymaster and sang it in his best midwestern voice. That song led to others. At midnight someone began the traditional "Auld Lang Syne" and with the last of the Tulagi Torpedoes held aloft the boys gave it a noble treatment.

They sat down. "I wonder," said Bernie O'Neill softly, "what the folks back home are doing right now."

Chapter Fourteen

THE SOC biplanes on Tulagi—a suicide pack if ever one existed—were doing everything in their power to make the long nights more endurable for the PT men. When there was moonlight these little planes, armed only with a single 30-caliber gun, patrolled the skies above the mosquito boats, maintaining radio contact and reporting anything of a suspicious nature in the vicinity.

For the men on the boats, this meant a relaxation of the frightful tension which now gripped their nerves whenever the little PTs went trouble hunting. If the Japs came down unannounced by far-reaching reconnaissance planes from Henderson Field, the SOCs could be relied upon to spot them.

Then over the torpedo boats' radios would come the warning: "There are enemy vessels in the vicinity . . ."

But the pilots had their troubles. Flying on moonlit nights they risked the danger of encountering enemy planes and could never be quite sure of an approaching plane's identity until, with their limited speed, it was too late to escape. And then, whether trouble sought them or not, there was always the grave peril of a crackup when landing in the dark on Tulagi harbor.

Two of these intrepid little planes were patrolling the skies above Tom Kendall's boat one night, while the PT beat back and forth on the Bitch Patrol. Aboard the boat, the men were not so tense as they would have been had not these winged eyes kept watch above.

The pilots' voices came up over the radio at regular intervals. "Everything okay. Everything still looks okay." Or: "Over Lengo Channel . . . no sign of trouble. Looks like you guys can postpone your expending for another night . . ."

On the PT boat, Crumpton grinned wearily at the skipper. "You know," he said, "it's a wonderful feeling, having those fellows up there. It's like having someone walk ahead of you through an alley on a dark night."

"It helps," Kendall agreed. "It sure does."

Then over Cavanah's radio came the voice of the first plane's pilot again, calling the other plane. A note of anxiety had crept into it.

"Is that you astern of me? Is that you astern?"

There was no immediate answer. The PT men, sensing drama in the misty darkness above, searched the sky for the two SOCs but could not see them.

"Is that you astern of me? *Answer, please!*"

There was an answer, but it was not the voice of the other pilot. Instead it was an angry chatter of machine-guns and the sudden shrill whine of a high-speed engine. Then silence.

Crumpton lowered his gaze and looked out over the water, lifting a hand to rub the lines of tension which had crept into his face.

LONG WERE THE NIGHTS

"That wasn't our other plane on his tail." He moistened his lips. "It was a Jap Zero."

On the second of January the Japs used their float-type Zeros on the PT boats to cover the approach of a destroyer task force. But it was a bad night for the experiment, a night wild with storm, and the planes were ineffective. Jack Searles and Les Gamble, Bernie O'Neill and Brent Greene and a pair of Squadron "R" boats knifed into the advancing destroyers and dispersed them, Gamble adding another certain torpedo hit to his impressive score.

On January 10 the enemy struck again, this time with a force which included at least one cruiser and seven destroyers. The weather, so often unreliable in that area of sudden drenching cloudbursts, was at its dismal worst, the sea and sky merged into a single limitless vale of ink. Down from the northwest swept a front of squalling clouds, now spurting wild sheets of rain, now settling wetly to smother the sea with mist.

The Japs rode the weather. Hidden in the advancing rain-front, they sped swiftly through the night toward their objective.

On the outer patrol, beyond Savo Island, four of the motor torpedo boats cruised doggedly back and forth, awaiting the enemy's coming. Tension was tremendous. Intelligence was convinced that the Japs would try new tactics in a desperate effort to thwart the thrusts of the mosquito boats, and reports at the operations office earlier in the eve-

LONG WERE THE NIGHTS

ning had been ominous.

It was late now. Beating the outer patrol with two boats from Squadron "T," Les Gamble and Bob Searles were worried. The men with the sharpest eyes stood lookout watch, crouched on the forward deck where the sea did its ugly best to smother them. The enemy, known to be on his way, was overdue. The night became more violent with each passing minute. If the Japs slipped through the outer patrol without being spotted, the PT striking force off the tip of Cape Esperance and Doma Reef might be caught without warning and trapped.

Aboard Gamble's boat, even Meadows could find nothing to be cheerful about as the gusty wind piled up waves that kept the craft drenched with spray. The little mosquito boat heaved and rocked. Waves boiled up in the darkness to break against the sloping windshield, and froth hissed white over the side to run gurgling along the torpedo tubes.

"It don't look so good, skipper," Meadows said, shaking his head. "It don't look good at all." He wiped the water from his eyes and glanced at the crouching forms of the lookouts up forward. "If those Japs have us figured out, they can sneak through within fifty yards of us without us seein' 'em."

The enemy may have had the PT patrols figured out, or it may have been pure luck. Whatever the answer, he rode the advancing storm center through the outer patrol undetected. And then, instead of rounding Savo Island on the north and beating down to the Guadalcanal shore at

[175]

Tassafaronga, the Jap force slipped south of Savo and was on top of the Cape Esperance patrol before the PTs in that area could be warned.

The three mosquito boats on that patrol, led by Lieutenant Westholm of Squadron "R," had been beating back and forth along the shore, handicapped by darkness which obliterated every landmark on the island. At slow speed they groped their way through the night, officers and men keyed to the point where nerves can break abruptly and talk is meaningless.

Suddenly the Japs were upon them—a long, swift line of enemy destroyers closing in to trap them against the shore.

There was no room to run. Over the radio came Westholm's voice, shrilling orders. "Attack! Attack! Break them up and go through them!" The squadron leader's boat showed the way, curling the sea white at her tail as she swung in a sharp turn to drive at the enemy line.

The other two turned with her, and in racing spread formation hit the Japs with all they had.

It was point-blank range. At least two of the destroyers were hit and fell out of formation. But the mosquito boats were outnumbered and caught in an impossible situation, their escape cut off by other Japs who rushed in for the kill. It was a little like a small-scale replica of the Battle of Guadalcanal, the night torn and gashed by torrents of gunfire and streaked with the gaudy comet-tails of tracer shells.

One Squadron "R" boat, scoring a hit, turned swiftly from the action and sped through the withering fire into the treacherous shoal water near the beach, where the Japs could not follow. With nothing to lose, she roared wide open along the beach and escaped. The others, with even that perilous route closed to them, tried valiantly to dash through the enemy formation as the Jap ships closed in about them. They had no chance to succeed. It was just a gesture.

Westholm's boat raced around a destroyer's stern, her gunners spraying the Jap with fire from all five guns. She was so close that the ricocheting tracers endangered her own men. Then a shell from another enemy ship burst on her bow and knocked most her crew sprawling, some with shrapnel wounds—but still she continued her desperate weaving and twisting through the enemy fleet.

That her men were not all killed by the six-inch shell which burst on her bow was a miracle. But with Westholm's hand on the wheel she found a crooked, fiery path through the enemy's converging lines and suddenly was through the gauntlet. When she sank, there was time to save her crew.

The other torpedo boat was less lucky. The Japs pocketed her. A criss-crossing avalanche of enemy fire burst about her and she was hit more than once. Still running, still darting desperately in search of an opening, she fled through a second torrent of fire to the beach and there ran aground. Her crew swam ashore.

But there were casualties. One man had been killed. Two others had been hurled into the sea by exploding shells.

Off Doma Reef, toward Lunga Point, the remaining three

PTs had been waiting tensely for some report from the outer patrol of the Japs' coming. Two were Squadron "X" boats —Jack Searles' and Stilly Taylor's. The other was a boat from "R."

When the Japs closed in on the Esperance patrol, these three heard the gunfire and saw the flashes and guessed what had happened. Leaving the "R" boat to cover the patrol area, Jack and Stilly raced up to take part in the action.

It was dark. The rain-front had passed, but the night was blacker, if possible, than before. Visibility was entirely dependent upon the lightning bursts of the battle raging off Esperance, and the two boats lost contact as they closed in.

A Jap searchlight came on, probing at the shore, where something lay beached at the water's edge.

"Skipper, look," said Kleinworth. "That's one of our boats." He handed Stilly the glasses.

Stilly looked. His lips thinned and he passed the glasses without comment to Teddy Kuharski. Then as the boat moved in to close with the enemy destroyer, every man aboard who could leave his post for a moment had a look at the white, broken thing in the beam of the Jap's searchlight.

"Skipper, that's Lieutenant Tilden's boat. They got Tilden."

"The bastards!"

"Those poor guys. You suppose they're dead, skipper?"

"We *got* to get that Jap. We can't miss!"

The PT moved in slowly, her engines throttled down for stealth. It was very dark, but now the dark was her ally.

The Jap inched his searchlight along the shore, and the flat bloom of brilliance whitened the sand and the grotesque stumps of shell-trimmed palms.

Lieutenant Dick Mahan, riding with Stilly as exec, lined the destroyer in the PT's sights. Wisdom stood ready on the torpedo firing circuit, his blunt face squared in a scowl. A few drops of rain fell. "Now!" Stilly said softly.

Three torpedoes ran. One stuck in the tube and began the infernal clatter of a hot run. But the crew was not interested in hot runs. Grimly, with hands clenched, they watched the Jap.

Suddenly on the destroyer's side appeared a soft red glow, then another—almost as though two invisible swimmers with their heads out of water had drawn deeply on a pair of glowing cigarettes. Then the red spots swelled. A rumbling explosion, long but not loud, flung the ship's stern from the sea.

The mosquito boat turned away, Wisdom clouting the stuck torpedo with his mallet. No one had cheered. No Jap destroyer—no Jap anything—could even the score for the riddled PT boat lying there on the Guadalcanal shore.

Chapter Fifteen

THE strangest sound in Maliali was the rumble of Count Basie's piano.

"You heard it at all hours," says Nick, "pounding from the native church—the islanders called it a 'God-house'—in which some of the men had set up a phonograph. The Count was a great uplifter in those trying times, and so were Fats Waller, Harry James and the rest of the swing-band leaders.

"The boys had quite a collection of records, including those which Tom Kendall and his crew had bought from the Marines, and whenever the thought of another red-dog or poker game made them slightly ill, they gathered in the church for a jam session. Hour after hour the phonograph ground out music—all kinds of music, sweet and swing, noisy and sentimental.

"The natives loved it. Some of them were still living in a section of the village, not minding our presence in the least, and when they heard the music they usually gathered around in great delight, soaking it up. Others came over to see what Doc Lastreto could do for them.

"They were sickly, most of them. Doc said they were suffering from yaws, a tropical skin-disease. Their faces and bodies were covered with running sores for which, apparently, they knew no cure, and when Doc out of pure human kindness began treating a few of them, he suddenly found himself with a full-sized clinic on his hands.

"It didn't faze Doc. He took over one of the shacks and turned it into a little hospital, and from then on, day or night, you were likely to see some of the locals lined up in front of his door for treatment.

"The natives loved him for it. They brought him all kinds of little offerings—fruit, vegetables, nuts—anything they could lay their hands on. And after a couple of weeks of Doc's treatments, they began to look a little less like candidates for the grave."

The native girls? Now and then from the tender the PT men had seen a few of them at a distance, but only two females showed up in Maliali the whole time they were there. One of these, wearing a basket on her head and little else, paraded past a shack in which some of the boys had set up housekeeping, and the rush to the window resembled a stampede to the fire-exits in a burning theater.

Tom Kendall won that race. "Boy!" he said. "Just like the *National Geographic!*"

But Maliali was a man's village, or else the native bucks did not trust the whites. The ladies were conspicuous by their absence.

A group of officers, including Greene, Kendall, the Searles brothers, Nikoloric, Taylor, Kernell and Mountcastle, had moved into an out-sized hut which at one time had been a native boat shop. It was not much but it was roomy, and when carpenters from the base force had cut in a pair of windows to admit some air, and built a deck to hold down the mud, it was practically a palace. It had a few drawbacks, however, the worst of which was spiders.

These were not tidy little back-home spiders, but enormous, shaggy brutes with bodies the size of golf-balls, covered with black hair. To each of them clung scores of tiny offspring, like ants swarming on a living ant-hill.

They were everywhere: on walls, floor and ceiling, in the men's cots, in discarded shoes and clothes, behind tubes of shaving-cream on the shelves. One of them resided permanently in a cranny just above Tom Kendall's bunk and came out daily to watch him while he slept.

Moon Mountcastle jeered at the boys' reluctance to associate with the hairy creatures. "You fellows worry too much," he said. To prove his point, he carelessly gathered one from his cot, carried it to the door and tossed it out. "See? Harmless," he insisted.

They eyed him dubiously. "Pure luck," said Bob. "Try it again and you'll probably get your hand eaten off!"

Mountcastle did it again. "Nothing to it," he declared. He was promptly and unanimously elected the squadron spider-catcher.

There were scorpions, too—swift, many-legged pests that lay in ambush under soiled clothes or beneath cot-sheets, only too willing to bite the unwary hand that disturbed them. But the spiders were the principal menace.

LONG WERE THE NIGHTS

"The man who objected most violently to those big black horrors," Bob recalls, "was Brent Greene. Brent could face the Japs any day without batting an eye, but big as he was, the spiders gave him the willies.

"He used to wake up in the night sometimes and find one of the brutes in bed with him, and then that high southern voice of his would sound forth like a siren, wailing for Mountcastle to come and remove the thing. Poor Moon—when he took that job of spider-catcher, he didn't know what he was letting himself in for. In the short time we lived at Maliali, he was the most popular guy on Tulagi."

But there was a brighter side to the picture, despite the spiders, the scorpions, and the need for constant bunk inspection. Despite, too, the limited food supply which consisted still of little else but canned spiced ham and corned beef with an occasional treat of vienna sausage.

About a thousand yards back of the village, a little jungle stream spilled over a bluff into a crystal pool that was right out of a South Sea movie. Here under the waterfall the men could bathe and wash their clothes in ice-cold water. It was a touch of paradise.

Later, the base force piped that water into the village and constructed a pair of showers. "It was heavenly," says Nick. "We used to stand there with that lovely cold water trickling down over the grime and the mosquito bites, and think of home. Anything was heavenly that induced thoughts of home. Because we had been out there then over three months, stalking the Japs night after night, losing weight and getting the jitters and wondering when, if ever, we'd be relieved.

"We knew we were not much good any more. Every man in the squadron knew it. Our efficiency had sunk to an all-time low, and the mere thought of another night of patrol gave us the horrors. It was so bad that none of us ever discussed the boats unless it was absolutely necessary. And when anything came along for a laugh or a touch of relief from that eternal tension, we literally pounced on it."

Like Joey Uptown. Joey—the PT men were responsible for his name—was a fuzzy-haired native who had volunteered for work one day in the hope of picking up a few odd pennies, though what he hoped to spend them on was a mystery. He spoke a mongrel English which some of the men understood sufficiently to converse with him.

For fifty cents a day, Joey agreed to keep the shack clean and do the laundry, also make the beds. But Joey was a man of enterprise. Do that kind of work with fifty cents in his pocket? Not Joey! He demanded his fifty cents daily in change—small change—and then promptly parceled out his chores to others who would do them for a nickel.

One day Joey shuffled into the "Officers' Club" with a pile of freshly scrubbed laundry in his arms, and after depositing his load on a cot, he plucked an undershirt off the top of it. The shirt was one of Stilly Taylor's. When tossed on the outgoing clothes pile it had been whole; now it was holey.

LONG WERE THE NIGHTS

"Shirt no good for wear dem sailor-fellers now, huh?" Joey suggested slyly, with an eye cocked at Stilly.

"Sure it is," Stilly said. "What's a little hole or two? Hand it over."

Joey frowned fiercely and shook his head. The shirt disappeared magically behind his back. "Shirt no good!" he insisted. "No good dem sailor-fellers. Only good Joey!" The scowl vanished. His mouth spread expansively in a grin, revealing very bad teeth stained red with betel-nut juice. "Shirt belong Joey now, huh?" he wheedled.

Stilly hesitated, shrugged, finally patted the little fellow's frowsy mop of hair. "The shirt is yours," Stilly said nobly. "Thus doth civilization find its way to the far corners of the earth."

Joey Uptown put it on—the shirt, not the civilization. Civilization was still a size or two beyond his reach.

He sat in the shack doorway, his bare feet crossed, a comb stuck in his hair, his bony chest encased in Stilly's undershirt and the rest of him wrapped in a giddy red skirt. Taking out his pipe, he stuffed it with sweet-smelling tobacco and contentedly began smoking. Over at the river bank, his hirelings were doing the washing.

Brent Greene came in. After thoroughly inspecting his cot for spiders, he stretched his big, athletic frame out on the sheets and went to sleep. Stilly was shaving. Tom Kendall was writing a letter.

Joey Uptown gazed peculiarly at Greene's fine head of hair and began to frown. Greene's hair was very blond, therefore greatly to be envied. Blond hair, which the natives achieved only by long and arduous treatment with lime juice, was the mark of an eligible bachelor. Joey had aspirations.

He wriggled closer, still closer, and at last timidly put out his hand to touch the object of his envy. Brent stirred and opened his eyes.

"Go away," Brent said sleepily.

Joey poked him again, this time in the chest.

"Go away," said Brent. "Go do the laundry."

Joey would not be dispersed. He stood up and leaned over the cot. "Sailor-feller tell Joey how can make hair pretty, huh?" he entreated. "Then Joey get wife do laundry!"

"You've already got half the village doing the laundry for you," Brent said. "What do you need a wife for?"

Joey heaved a sigh. These Americans, they were nice fellers but dumb. Oh, so dumb! "Wife," said Joey, "do laundry for nothing!"

Bernie O'Neill and Doc Lastreto were enthusiastic sightseers. Occasionally, when they took mail or passengers over to Guadalcanal and found themselves with a few odd hours to kill, they fought with the Marines at the front. On other occasions they went along on bombing raids. On still others they took trips of the quiet tourist variety, visiting the native villages on Tulagi.

In these jungle villages the islanders were as friendly

toward the Americans as were those in Maliali. Yet these were the same natives who not long ago had fled in terror from the Japs, and during the Japs' stay on the island had remained in hiding, fearful of their lives.

Why were they not afraid of the Americans? "Perhaps," says Bob, "because we paid them whenever they pitched in to lend us a hand—though what they hoped to do with the money we never could figure out. Maybe they just liked us."

At the base, the enlisted men tinkered with the *Stinky Maru*, the little Jap gig found drifting in Sleepless Lagoon. It would have made a first-class utility boat. But the *Stinky* remained loyal to the enemy. Its tiny inboard engine, built apparently of old tin cans and scrap, finally broke down completely, and with no spare parts on hand the men were unable to repair it.

Meanwhile the patrols went on and men's nerves became more and more ragged.

"Those nights toward the end," Bob says, "were the worst of all. The boats were almost all in bad shape from overwork and lack of replacement parts. Our speed was gone, and the Japs knew exactly where we were.

"If we could have shuffled our patrols around a bit it would have helped, but the topography of the area was such that this was impossible. The Jap bases were all northwest of us, and the enemy ships always came in the same way—down through the slot to Savo Island, then around Savo on their way to the Guadalcanal shore.

"Therefore we had to maintain outer patrols beyond Savo to spot them on the way down, and inner patrols off Cape Esperance, Kamimbo Bay and Tassafaronga to intercept them. There was simply no other place for us to lie in wait if we hoped to be of any use.

"The Japs knew this as well as we did, and consequently we were no longer able to surprise them. They were always alert, always ready for us. We had to go at them with only the darkness for protection, our engines fouled from the everlasting grind of slow-speed patrolling.

"It was hell on the engineers. On Tom Kendall's boat, for instance, one of the engines had seen more than eight hundred hours of service. Other boats could almost equal that record. Yet the boys kept things going by working themselves half to death down there in the awful heat and din of the engine-rooms.

"Nelson, one of Tom's machinist's mates, used to work until he dropped. He was so sick one night in the midst of an action that he couldn't stay on his feet, yet when one of the engines went bad because of a balky carburetor, Nelson got hold of a wobble-pump—a gadget for souping the gas supply—and kept that troublesome engine going until the boat was out of danger. He postponed his collapsing until later.

"Peterson was the same. The carbon monoxide fumes knocked him out once for twenty minutes. This was on Stilly's boat. Stilly told him, 'For God's sake, Pete, take it easy!' But Peterson just grinned at him and went back to work.

"All the men were the same. They worked day and night. Some of them were old-timers and hadn't been home in a long while. Elvie O'Daniel, Tom's torpedoman, had served out in the China Station and hadn't seen his wife in almost two years. Ray Long carried his baby's picture around and used to look at it on the sly when he thought no one was watching him. You could go right down the list, naming man after man—their duties were pure hell and they just about killed themselves to keep the boats in operation.

"We relied on these men, all of them. Without them we never could have kept going. They in turn looked to us for leadership and inspiration, and at the top of the whole show were Robbie and Jack."

"In those last weeks," says Nick, "with more than half the men sick and the boats being kept in commission with spit and a prayer, Robbie literally held the entire outfit together with his guidance and understanding. Then he joined the staff of Commander Calvert, who had become commanding officer of the entire PT flotilla, and Jack Searles became C.O. of Squadron 'X.'

"Jack, too, held us together. Our efficiency was gone, our nerves were frayed all to pieces and in plain one-syllable language we were scared. Yet the patrols continued night after night without let-up and somehow we managed to keep the Japs from getting their troops and supplies ashore.

Or anyway, we slowed them up and made it mighty tough for them."

The enemy was wary these January nights. His strength had been whittled down and his attempts to supply his troops on Guadalcanal had been frustrated time and again. He changed his tactics. Instead of trying to bull his way through the watchful PT boats, he now began sending in single swift destroyers which raced through the PT patrols and fled out again, leaving behind stores and ammunition which had been flung overboard to float ashore.

But the mosquito boats thwarted this move, too. At dawn they beat back and forth along the coast of Japland, located the floating drums and riddled them with machine-gun fire. The Japs on Guadalcanal were going hungry.

Then on the night of January 14, the enemy in desperation tried again to land reinforcements. With the elements providing a backdrop of storm and lightning, he sent a force of at least nine destroyers and two cargo ships.

The PTs were waiting, Hugh Robinson in command.

It was a brief action, lit luridly by nature's fireworks. Lightning revealed the enemy's movements, silhouetting his ships against the sprawling shadows of Guadalcanal as he endeavored to creep in along the island's shore.

The mosquito boats picked their targets and attacked. Torpedoes found their marks. With the thunder boats driving at them in groups of three from three directions, the disorganized Japs turned tail and fled.

Chapter Sixteen

FOR the Japs, this was the end. The action itself may not have been of major significance, but if the enemy ships had been sent into the area as a feeler force, as appears probable, the information they took back to Bougainville was no more heartening than that delivered by other reconnaissance groups in the past.

The angry waters between Guadalcanal and Tulagi were still patrolled, still perilous. The motor torpedo boats were still there.

The Japs could afford to risk no more of their ships and men in luckless nighttime attempts to rebuild their strength on Guadalcanal. The cost had been too great. Time and again for more than four months the enemy's infiltration fleets had been set upon and dispersed—more often with serious damage than without—by the ceaselessly vigilant PTs.

Jap troops on the island were starving. They lacked supplies and ammunition and were hopelessly in need of reinforcement. With increasing vigor, as the PT boats kept the Bougainville Express at bay and American troops on the island caught up on their sleep, the Japs had been mauled in their attempts to close in on Henderson Field.

Fresh army troops had replaced many of the heroic Marines on the island. Jap headquarters at Kokumbona, the

LONG WERE THE NIGHTS

pulsing heart of Japland, was under assault and on January 25 was captured in a smashing, deadly attack. The Japs who for months had been entrenched on Cape Esperance were then outflanked. The end was near.

The island itself was a shambles. Between Lunga Point and Esperance the white sands were littered with the wreckage of Jap transports and landing barges, some of them smashed in the great naval battles of November, others by the night-prowling torpedo boats. East of Henderson Field were more of them: desolate, charred hulks scattered along the beach as though flung there by hurricane. The washed-up bodies of their crews had been buried by the hundreds, and still others were left for burial by every receding tide.

The island? The Japs now called it "Death Island" because so many of them had perished there—or in trying to get there. It had been beautiful once, though American fighting men will not believe it. Perhaps it will be a tropical paradise again. But now in those early days of February it was a place of death, its earth churned and sodden, its palm groves blasted to stumps by artillery and mortar fire. Rude crosses marked the graves of the men who had died to take and defend it. At the mouth of the Matanikau River, where that peaceful stream ran broadly from the Guadalcanal jungle, Jap tanks lay twisted and broken in silent testimony to the ferocity of the enemy's vain struggle to reach his objective.

Henderson Field was still American. The Japs on the island had been squeezed into small, tight pockets of last-ditch resistance. The Guadalcanal War was about over, and in the making—or already made—was an American epic of heroism which would stand proudly on a peak of history.

The motor torpedo boats, small, savage instruments of attack and attrition, had played a noble part in that epic, and were to play a valiant though tragic part in its finale. For when the Japs gave up the fight and began their evacuation of Guadalcanal on February first, the PT boats were the only American naval force to be sent against them.

The PT men did not know the Japs were abandoning the disputed island that night. For them it was just another night of patrol, more terrible than some of the preceding ones because reconnaissance had reported an enemy fleet of great size in the slot. At least twenty destroyers, the report said, were moving down from the Jap bases in the northwest.

The PTs deployed to meet them, while planes from Guadalcanal, searching for the enemy fleet in the dark, found part of it and fought a bitter battle with a swarm of covering Zeros. In that brief, slashing conflict, two of the Jap destroyers were sunk, another damaged. Some American planes were lost.

The rest of the enemy fleet came on.

Eleven of the little thunder boats were on guard that night. In the dark, tense and expectant, they beat back and forth awaiting the enemy. The odds against them were formidable, to put it mildly. In more than one man's mind was the grim thought that now, if never before, he had been marked down as expendable. Fervently they hoped that the inky blackness of the night itself would provide them with some small measure of surprise with which to combat the Japs' almost certain knowledge of their presence.

The Squadron "X" men on patrol that night were not the men who had so confidently sent their little boats against the enemy's forces in October and November. Only their names remained the same. Physically and mentally they were worn out. For a long time they had seen their efficiency ebbing, little mistakes and errors of judgment cropping up in tired, sick men who never before had blundered. Their timing was off. Of late they had been fumbling into the enemy instead of stalking him and closing with deadly sureness for the attack.

They had had enough. Their courage remained unimpaired, but human endurance had reached the breaking point. Tonight as they crept through the dark with feelers extended, they watched with haunted eyes and prayed that the attacking American planes might turn the enemy back.

The Japs came on. Ahead of them sped a formation of float Zeros, whose pilots at once spread out to sweep the danger area. The area itself had been overworked and drained of all cover by four months of nocturnal fighting.

Screaming above the PT patrols, the Zeros struck savagely with machine-guns, slashing the night with tracer fire. Their fire was wild, their attack ineffectual, but they were a nuisance. While they returned time and again in a frantic attempt to strafe the torpedo boats, the overwhelming force of warships deployed to attack. The action everywhere was wild and violent.

Southwest of Savo Island a Squadron "T" boat tossed the sea from her bow in a headlong slash at the destroyer force as the latter rushed into the combat zone. The Japs were not expecting an attack from that quarter. Their attention was focused on the tracer fireworks off Esperance, where the Zeros had momentarily located Jack Searles and a Squadron "R" boat.

The "T" boat, commanded by Lieutenant Clark Faulkner, had her choice of half a score of targets and picked the nearest destroyer. She fired, then turned and ran without having been seen. Behind her the Jap warship blazed from a hit and limped out of line.

The other PTs found conditions less favorable. Under a sky full of enemy planes they dodged bombs now, as well as machine-gun fire, while maneuvering into position to attack the enemy fleet. Harassed and outnumbered two to one by Jap destroyers, they nevertheless did their brave best to thwart the enemy's mission.

A Zero screamed down upon Ensign Richards' boat of Squadron "T" as she bellowed in to strike at the head of the destroyer column. The PT's guns kept the attacking plane at bay, but the destroyer itself opened fire at close range. The mosquito boat turned at top speed to find another angle of attack, her 20-mm. chattering a defiant answer to the Jap's heavier weapons. A shell fell squarely on her deck.

LONG WERE THE NIGHTS

For a moment the stricken boat circled aimlessly, her plywood hull ablaze and the flames reaching for her gas tanks, while those of her crew who had not been killed by the exploding shell struggled dazedly to abandon ship. Six succeeded. A few minutes later they saw their boat slide stern first into the flame-reddened sea. She did not explode; she just disappeared. In the dark the survivors made for Savo Island and reached safety.

Ensign Jimmy Kelly's boat, of Squadron "R," zigzagged under the strafing Zeros and ran into a closing circle of warships. The planes' tracers pursued her. Searchlights on the destroyers stabbed out their blinding beams to pin her down, and 4.7s thundered at her from three directions. One of them exploded in her fuel tanks.

Her men on deck were killed, and all but one of her engine-room crew perished in the blast that tore the boat apart. He, blown through the side of the boat, was picked up by another PT the following morning.

Jap planes screamed in the sky. Jap destroyers—nearly a score of them—covered the waters of Sleepless Lagoon in a vast parade, their boiling wakes crossing and recrossing in the dark. There was no longer a plan of attack for either the Japs or the torpedo boats. The battle had burst apart into swift, vicious dog-fights and the night was a red hell of gunfire that shook the neighboring islands with its fury.

Bob Searles and Stilly Taylor had been southeast of Savo when the inferno erupted. Officers and men on both boats, grimly awaiting the word from the outer patrol, had known what they faced and were glumly aware that the impending clash between giants and Lilliputians might be their last.

In the heat of the engine-room, Beed and Winter worked frantically over the engines, doing what they could, even then, to ready them for the moment when those worn-out hulks of temperamental machinery would be called on for all they possessed.

All they possessed? These Jap destroyers pouring into the area could do thirty-five knots or more, and were numerous enough to cover the whole region between Guadalcanal and Tulagi without leaving a loophole. With luck, the PT might be able to outrun them still, despite her fouled engines. But her engineers, sweating below deck, wiped their oily faces with oily hands and glumly shook their heads.

"We'll get it," Winter said. "That many ships—we haven't got a chance."

Lorran Beed, always quiet, said nothing. There was nothing to say.

The boat beat slowly on its patrol, Bob Searles at the wheel and Bill Kreiner anxiously searching the night for the flashes of gunfire which would indicate the enemy's arrival. They knew, even better than the men knew, that against such a multitude of Jap ships their chance of victory, even of survival, was terribly small. And with this knowledge was a feeling of hopelessness that the nocturnal hell in Sleepless Lagoon would go on forever, no matter what happened on Guadalcanal.

"We'd heard about the fall of Jap headquarters at Kokumbona," Bob recalls, "and how the Japs on Esperance were hopelessly pocketed. Yet here was this armada of enemy ships steaming down, and we didn't know why they were coming or what they hoped to accomplish, and everyone had the feeling that our part of the fighting was never going to end. Night after night for the rest of our lives we'd be doing this all over again, until the men cracked and the boats fell completely to pieces."

Edwards and Lueckert, on the 50-caliber guns, were wedged in their turrets waiting for trouble, their knuckles white, faces creased with tension tracks. Bockemuehl waited rigidly at the radio. No one talked. Off to port and a little astern, Stilly Taylor and his crew were prowling along, too, in this dread game of David and the Goliaths, and Bob Searles' men could see her wake shining white in the dark, and it was comforting.

Where were the Japs?

Suddenly above the mutter of the boat's engines the men heard the sharper, shriller sound of airplane motors in the murk above. Air attack! They looked up, faces white with strain. The gunners swung the snouts of their weapons up and nervously felt for the unseen enemy. Bill Kreiner turned to the skipper and shook his head.

"We're really going to get it. But good," Bill said.

Then a Jap Zero was over them, a speeding dark shadow against the sky's deeper darkness. Machine-guns chattered. Garish fingers of tracer fire stabbed down at the swerving boat as Bob spun the wheel and jammed the throttles up.

Close, very close, were the little bubbling spurts of spray tossed up by the sea as the Jap's bullets missed the boat and swept in line astern of her. Close, too, was the snarling fire of the PT as her guns swung swiftly to follow the marauding shadow in its flight. Then the plane circled, swept in again.

A second Zero had spotted the PT and was reaching for her with tracers, and now as the two boats zigzagged at high speed and their gunners sent burst after burst into the sky, enemy destroyers loomed up in the dark, trapped the darting craft in their searchlights and loosed a torrent of shells.

Three times the two speeding PTs were strafed. Three times the Zeros swarmed down in the dark, screamed over them with guns raggedly spitting flame, while the enemy ships thundered salvo after salvo of 4.7s.

It was too hot a corner for the little thunder boats. They fled, returning the fire as they ran. Through the destroyer screen they flew, so close that the bursts of flame from the ships' turrets lit the gaunt, tired faces of the men.

Behind the Japs lay Savo Island with its treacherous shoal waters and dark pockets of concealment. The two boats scurried for this haven, weaving and twisting to dodge the enemy's torrent of fire while their overworked engines labored hoarsely and the destroyers pressed after them like swift greyhounds. Even against those worn-out, patched-up engines the Japs were not quite fast enough.

The black knobs of Savo loomed ahead, and Bob Searles sent the PT grumbling toward them. In and out among the little upthrust lumps of land offshore the boat zigzagged, while Kreiner and Meadows shouted out the dangers. Behind came Stilly Taylor's boat, the sea curling white under her bow and tracing a broad white snake at her tail.

The Zeros had swarmed away, finding the PTs' fire too vicious, but shellfire from the destroyers pursued the torpedo boats to the last. Then the two Squadron "X" boats were safe, thanks to the skill and daring of their skippers and the courage of shaken men who had stuck to their guns, pouring out a murderous fire to keep the Japs at bay.

But they were out of the fight, trapped in Savo's shadows. Out in Sleepless Lagoon the fantastic battle of pygmies and giants was reaching its furious climax.

Of the huge Jap fleet, apparently only four or five destroyers had been assigned to evacuate troops—probably officers—from the narrow Jap beachhead on Guadalcanal. The rest had been sent down, with air coverage which proved ineffective, to try to protect the evacuation ships from attack by the PT boats. A subtle compliment indeed to the aggressive and greatly feared little thunder-bugs!

Now these five Jap destroyers were lined up along the shore, dark shapes against the island's shadows, while landing boats sped back and forth between them and the beach. Defense in depth made it extremely difficult for the PTs to attack them.

Jack Searles' boat, assailed by Zeros off the tip of Cape Esperance, nevertheless made a courageous attempt to strike at the warships near the beach. The Zeros pursued her. Osborne and Happy Parker, on her machine-guns, sent all they had at the swarming planes, but their task was almost hopeless.

These men were expert gunners. They had proved it in earlier actions. But those swift, dark shadows in the midnight sky were mere ghosts of targets, invisible until directly overhead and then gone before the snouts of the PT's guns could be swung to center them. Then the screening destroyers opened fire and the boat turned away. With Jack Searles at the wheel and Al Snowball grimly searching for a route of escape, she roared north and east toward Savo Island.

Suddenly she was surrounded by a second swarm of destroyers!

"Three of them!" Snowball shouted. "Four—five—six— good God, they're still coming down from Bougainville!"

But something else was coming down from Bougainville. The Japs were up to their old trick of using the weather for a shield. A sudden blinding rain squall, less than half a mile wide and probably no more than that in depth, swept in to smother the trapped PT. The Japs had been steaming down behind it. A quirk of the wind, a trick of that always tricky Solomon Islands weather, had flung the rain center ahead of them and now the mosquito boat was smothered in a drenching cloud-burst.

That was all Jack Searles needed. Estimating the speed of the squall, he turned the boat with it. Under a heaven-sent cone of cover she slipped through the enemy fleet and shook off pursuit, escaping almost certain destruction.

Then her luck ran out. The squall passed; the night was clear again. No longer seeking to escape, but circling to close for action, the torpedo boat was suddenly pinned like a moth in the beam of a searchlight.

She had run into still another swarm of warships. They were all about her. Their lights reached out, swung back and forth, converged on the little boat and held her.

The PT's guns spat a staccato fire at the lights to smash them, but the Japs had turned their heaviest guns on her. The sea erupted in huge columns of water not thirty yards from the weaving boat.

There was only one move left. Even that would require the aid of a miracle. These men had fought too well for too long to be sacrificed in a futile attempt to continue the fight against such tremendous odds. Like Stilly Taylor and Bob Searles before him, Jack again turned the nose of his boat toward Savo Island, the nearest place of refuge, and with her engines called on for every ounce of their limited speed the little boat ran the gauntlet.

Through the converging destroyers she ripped and slashed her way, and at full speed ran up on Savo's sands—the third mosquito boat to find refuge on the tiny island since the start of the battle.

Few of the PTs were left in action. South of Esperance, a Squadron "T" boat had made a brave but futile effort to close the warships evacuating troops, and was at once attacked by Zeros and destroyers. The voice of her radioman came up over the air in a frantic bellow at the height of the action.

"My God, the whole Jap fleet's on our tail!"

Fired on from all sides, strafed by the angry Zeros, the boat cut a zigzag, crazy course across Sleepless Lagoon until she, too, found the blessed haven of Savo Island.

Two miles southwest of Savo, the Jap fleet had closed in on a Squadron "R" boat captained by Lieutenant Johnny Clagett and the boat in command of the ace scorer of Squadron "X," Les Gamble.

Clagett had no chance. The Japs were on him; the trap closed before he could escape. Caught in a flood of searchlights, with enemy ships snarling about him like hounds about a holed fox, he nevertheless loosed a torpedo before attempting his suicidal run for freedom.

There was nowhere to run. The big Jap guns ranged on the fleeing boat, pouring shell after shell at her as she turned at top speed from one blocked lane of escape to another, until at last an enemy battery found the mark and a shell burst on her deck.

Still running, but at slow speed now with two of her three engines demolished, the doomed boat was engulfed by flames. Clagett himself, severely burned, stayed at her wheel, guiding the flaming comet through the night while the Japs, sure that she was done for, turned their fire on Les Gamble.

But Clagett was not through. In the few moments still left

to him he took his dying boat close enough to Savo so that when she sank, those of her crew who still lived were able to swim to safety.

Les Gamble, caught in that same trap, with the night an erupting volcano of destroyer fire and strafing planes, won a smile from Fate by his boldness. No tactician would have given him a chance. His PT was caught in an impossible situation, a Jap ship bearing down on her to port, a second Jap closing in at top speed to starboard. Between the two, the torpedo boat maneuvered dizzily in an ever narrowing space, to escape the fire of both destroyers' batteries and a screeching machine-gun assault from the sky.

But the PT still had some of her speed, and down in her engine-room Gilgore and Johnson fought the fumes and heat to add thunder to the roar of her engines. When Sid Rabekoff thumbed the throttles, the little craft responded.

Gamble knew what he was doing, even though it could not by all logic be done. Under his breath he swore fluently. At the fifties, Beckers and Hummer poured their fire into the closing destroyers as the PT took off.

Straight for the nearer ship Gamble sent his boat, her wake a broad white gash visible to the enemy. Her guns chattered a noisy challenge. Her engines bellowed. She was on collision course with all the speed she had.

The Jap saw her coming and swerved. In swerving, he opened a lane of escape and Gamble swung the boat through it.

Dead ahead was Savo Island, center of all the action that

night and shelter for those boats which, after attacking, had been lucky enough to escape through the many arms of the Octopus. With the two destroyers in angry pursuit and others wheeling to join in the chase, Gamble sent the fleeing boat straight for the island's shore.

Not until the last minute, when the black peaks of Savo seemed about to totter onto the boat's deck, did she slacken speed. Through shoal water she skittered, tossing clouds of spray astern. Then her nose bit the beach and with a last sullen growl of her engines, she stopped.

Her men swarmed over the side and splashed ashore, through enemy fire that sought for them in a fury of frustration. Rabekoff followed, urging the skipper to hurry.

For a moment Gamble stood knee-deep in water by his boat, facing the Jap's fire while searchlights felt through the dark toward him. Then with a shake of his head the high-scoring skipper of Squadron "X" turned away.

The battle was over.

It was the end. Once more the Japs came down from their northern bases to evacuate their beaten, starving troops from Guadalcanal, but the PT fleet was not ordered out to engage them. Their work was finished. On Guadalcanal, the enemy's remaining troops were rounded up, and on February 8 all fighting ceased.

Over that bloody battle area, where for six explosive months the Japs had struggled with all the strength at their command to reclaim what had been snatched from them, now hung a strange, deathlike quiet. American troops buried the enemy dead—and their own. The sea washed up the wreckage of shell-blasted ships. The men of the motor torpedo boat squadrons towed their disabled boats back to base and worked to repair them. They thought they might have to use them again.

They didn't. The Guadalcanal campaign was finished.

Chapter Seventeen

WHAT, after all, had Squadron "X" accomplished? What was the score?

The navy, ever conservative, credits the eight midget mosquito boats of the squadron with the certain sinking of a heavy cruiser, six destroyers, a submarine and two or three smaller craft, in four months of action.

The line of little Jap flags on the PT emblem at Sesapi was longer than that. Much longer than that. But the PTs fought at night. Striking with the speed and surprise of lightning bolts, they were often racing wide open for home before the results of their attacks could be determined.

Without doubt the flags on the PT emblem tell a more accurate story than the conservative official figures. But does it matter?

"We thought it did," said Lieutenant Commander Alan Montgomery, his fingers tautly drumming the desk in the PT Shakedown Office. "It's only fair, I think, to admit that when our part in the Guadalcanal campaign was over and we weighed the hell of those long, long nights against what the navy said we had accomplished, we were disappointed.

"Then, cooling, we began to see the picture as a whole and to realize that we had been sent out there to do a certain specific job, and had done it. I think we did it fairly well. I think the Japs will remember us."

LONG WERE THE NIGHTS

The Japs will remember them. And so, in a different way, will those Guadalcanal Marines who, until the PT boats arrived to derail the Bougainville Express, had been pounded mercilessly night after night when they wanted sleep.

It is true that in the grand finale the little thunder boats of Squadron "X" encountered an overwhelming force of the enemy at a time when their own efficiency was ebbing. But their record of achievement over four long months of grueling combat cannot be weighed against the results of one suicidal attack against an enemy fleet of such proportions. They are marauders, not mammoths.

Their work is of a specialized character. Provided with suitable bases from which they can operate with some element of surprise—provided also with the necessary replacement parts for their fragile hulls and high-speed engines—they are able to hit harder, with less expenditure of men and money, than any other branch of sea-power.

They are the best and often the only answer to nocturnal infiltration. On patrol, no other craft can cover so large an area under such conditions and at the same time so savagely attack the enemy's greatest might.

The conditions under which Squadron "X" fought may never be repeated, for the tide of war is turning now. These men, like the Marines who took and held Guadalcanal, had to work with what little they had and what little could be brought in to them. The bringing was difficult. Their boats were not new in the beginning and were kept in operation only with enormous effort. There were never enough of them.

Today, in the Solomons and elsewhere, newer, faster torpedo boats are in service: boats with the speed to outrun with ease the swiftest ships the enemy can send against them, and with replacement parts to keep them at peak efficiency.

Yet Squadron "X," with but eight midget motor boats, ruled the nights in Sleepless Lagoon. That is the culminal triumph for which Montgomery's nocturnal marauders will be remembered.

. . . .

The Guadalcanal War was over. The Japs had been liquidated. One day a guard-mail boat slipped into Tulagi harbor while Nick was standing on the dock.

The skipper stepped ashore with a slip of paper in his hand. "I think I may have some news," he said, "for you guys in 'X.'"

Nick took the slip of paper and unfolded it. He studied it a long time, then looked up over the blue, smooth waters of Sleepless Lagoon, where for so many endless nights the little thunder boats of Squadron "X" had battled the best the Japs could send. The sun was a golden haze over Guadalcanal, feeling out the dark shadows under her rugged peaks.

Nick turned away and began walking, then running. At the base he burst into the radio shack, where officers and

LONG WERE THE NIGHTS

men were awaiting the night's orders. Wildly he waved the paper.

But he did not shout the news after all. It refused to be yelled. The words when they came were spoken quietly.

"Fellows," Nick said, "we're being relieved."

Officers and Enlisted Personnel of PT Squadron "X"

SQUADRON COMMANDER
* LIEUTENANT COMMANDER ALAN R. MONTGOMERY
  Warrenton, Va.

* ° LIEUTENANT LESTER H. GAMBLE
  San Francisco, Cal.
* LIEUTENANT (JG) JAMES BRENT GREENE
  Frankfort, Ky.
  LIEUTENANT (JG) JOHN F. KEARNEY
  West Englewood, N.J.
  LIEUTENANT THOMAS E. KENDALL, JR.
  Minneapolis, Minn.
  LIEUTENANT (JG) JOSEPH C. KERNELL
  Beverly Hills, Cal.
  LIEUTENANT (JG) WILLIAM E. KREINER, III
  Buffalo, N.Y.
* LIEUTENANT (JG) LEONARD A. NIKOLORIC
  Englewood, N.J.
  LIEUTENANT (JG) BERNARD J. O'NEILL
  Baltimore, Md.
* LIEUTENANT HUGH M. ROBINSON
  Squadron Executive Officer
  Springfield, Mass.
  LIEUTENANT (JG) WILLIAM J. RYAN
  Hartford, Conn.
° LIEUTENANT JOHN MALCOLM SEARLES
  Leonia, N.J.

* Awarded Silver Star.
° Awarded Navy Cross.

* Lieutenant Robert L. Searles
   Leonia, N.J.
* Lieutenant Henry S. Taylor
   Cold Spring Harbor, L.I., N.Y.
Lieutenant (jg) Stanley C. Thomas
   Bethlehem, Penn.
Lieutenant Robert C. Wark
   Portland, Ore.

Eldon R. Alvis, Chief Radioman
   Brooklyn, N.Y.
* Lee A. Bagby, Quartermaster, 1st Class
   Red Bluff, Cal.
Robert C. Barnard, Machinist's Mate, 1st Class
   Jackson, Mich.
Roy L. Beckers, Gunner's Mate, 1st Class
   Mount Pulaski, Ill.
Lorran E. Beed, Chief Machinist's Mate
   Brooklyn, N.Y.
Robert H. Blackwood, Gunner's Mate, 2nd Class
   Aurora, Ill.
George D. Bockemuehl, Radioman, 2nd Class
   Minneapolis, Minn.
Henry D. Bracy, Baker, 1st Class
   Detroit, Mich.
Nicholas F. Carideo, Ship's Cook, 1st Class
   Erie, Penn.
Charles R. Carner, Chief Motor Machinist's Mate
   Charleston, S.C.
Woodrow W. Cavanah, Radioman, 1st Class
   Rocky Ford, Colo.

* Awarded Silver Star.

Otis Cline, Chief Machinist's Mate
    Carterville, Mo.
Marvin I. Crosson, Chief Torpedoman
    Fort Worth, Tex.
Ralph H. Crumpton, Chief Quartermaster
    Houston, Tex.
John Der, Motor Machinist's Mate, 1st Class
    Akron, Ohio
* George W. Ebersberger, Jr., Mo. Mach. Mate, 1st Class
    Pittsburgh, Penn.
Eldon E. Edwards, Chief Gunner's Mate
    San Diego, Cal.
Harlan E. Gilgore, Machinist's Mate, 1st Class
    Lancaster, Penn.
George W. Gilpin, Radioman, 1st Class
    Mobile, Ala.
Brenton E. Goddard, Chief Torpedoman
    Jamaica Plain, Mass.
Gavin J. Hamilton, Chief Radioman
    Point Clear, Ala.
Lloyd V. Hummer, Ship's Cook, 1st Class
    Plainfield, N.J.
James L. Jeans, Machinist's Mate, 1st Class
    Eugene, Ore.
Clifton P. Johnson, Chief Motor Machinist's Mate
    Raymond, N.H.
* Harold C. Johnson, Chief Quartermaster
    Portsmouth, Va.
Charles M. Kiefer, Machinist's Mate, 1st Class
    Eldorado Springs, Mo.
Boyd G. Kleinworth, Chief Quartermaster
    Fullerton, Cal.

* Awarded Silver Star.

Joseph M. Koval, Chief Commissary Steward
    Central Falls, R.I.
Teddy S. Kuharski, Gunner's Mate, 1st Class
    New Castle, Penn.
* John D. Legg, Chief Quartermaster
    San Antonio, Tex.
Ray H. Long, Machinist's Mate, 1st Class
    Boston, Mass.
Stephen J. Lott, Jr., Torpedoman, 1st Class
    Richmond Hill, L.I., N.Y.
Scottie D. Lueckert, Chief Torpedoman
    San Diego, Cal.
Ivah C. May, Chief Commissary Steward
    Warrington, Fla.
James T. Meadows, Jr., Chief Quartermaster
    Wilmington, N.C.
Stephen A. Mehes, Ship's Cook, 1st Class
    Perth Amboy, N.J.
Leon O. Nale, Gunner's Mate, 1st Class
    Pine Hill, Ala.
William C. Nelson, Machinist's Mate, 1st Class
    Fountain Inn, S.C.
Joseph V. Nemec, Machinist's Mate, 1st Class
    Buffalo, N.Y.
Alfred R. Norwood, Chief Torpedoman
    West Roxbury, Mass.
Elvie J. O'Daniel, Chief Torpedoman
    Hopkinsville, Ky.
Frank O'Malley, Ship's Cook, 2nd Class
    Detroit, Mich.
* Cletus E. Osborne, Gunner's Mate, 1st Class
    San Francisco, Cal.

* Awarded Silver Star.

DeWayne H. Parker, Motor Machinist's Mate, 1st Class
   Fort Wayne, Ind.
* Benjamin F. Parrish, Gunner's Mate, 1st Class
   Castalia, N.C.
Owen S. Pearle, Chief Radioman
   Brooklyn, N.Y.
Howard P. Peterson, Chief Machinist's Mate
   Lincoln, Neb.
Lester A. Piper, Chief Radioman
   Beaverdam, Ohio
Alsie A. Porterfield, Chief Machinist's Mate
   Benton, Ark.
Willie E. Purvis, Radioman, 1st Class
   El Dorado, Ark.
Henry M. Ramsdell, Chief Machinist's Mate
   Orlando, Fla.
Thomas R. Ratcliff, Machinist's Mate, 1st Class
   McAllen, Tex.
Kenneth R. Sawyer, Quartermaster, 1st Class
   Louisville, Ky.
Clarence Schrock, Chief Quartermaster
   Columbus, Ohio
Oliver Shaw, Chief Motor Machinist's Mate
   Columbus, Ohio
* Emil P. Stayonovich, Torpedoman, 2nd Class
   Lima, Ohio
Theodore B. Stephens, Motor Machinist's Mate, 1st Class
   Cuyahoga Falls, Ohio
Paul L. Stephenson, Radioman, 1st Class
   St. Paul, Minn.
Arthur Stuffert, Chief Machinist's Mate
   Plainfield, N.J.

* Awarded Silver Star.

Carl E. Todd, Ship's Cook, 1st Class
   Brooklyn, N.Y.
William F. Uhl, Chief Torpedoman
   Bethlehem, Penn.
William J. Winter, Jr., Chief Machinist's Mate
   Alameda, Cal.
Hobert D. Wisdom, Chief Torpedoman
   Centerview, Mo.
* Stephen Yando, Motor Machinist's Mate, 1st Class
   Detroit, Mich.

* Awarded Silver Star.

BASE FORCE

Lieutenant (jg) Emilio D. Lastreto
  San Francisco, Cal.
Lieutenant (jg) Lorenzo Torres
  Tulsa, Okla.

James H. Archbold, Jr., Shipfitter, 3rd Class
  Los Angeles, Cal.
Henry C. Benton, Torpedoman, 3rd Class
  Goldsboro, N.C.
Maloy R. Bills, Gunner's Mate, 1st Class
  Riverton, Utah
John T. Burns, Chief Motor Machinist's Mate
  Ancon, Canal Zone
George H. Coberth, Machinist's Mate, 1st Class
  Arlington, Va.
Clay O. Cotton, Chief Machinist's Mate
  Leslie, Ark.
David A. Covellone, Chief Machinist's Mate
  Los Angeles, Cal.
* Harold C. Crouch, Machinist's Mate, 2nd Class
  Bedford, Va.
Thomas A. Dufresne, Electrician's Mate, 1st Class
  Missoula, Mont.
Charles E. Farrar, Electrician's Mate, 3rd Class
  Ingleside, W.Va.
Robert E. Golden, Chief Storekeeper
  Noroton Heights, Conn.
Elkins Grove, Chief Machinist's Mate
  Huntington, W.Va.

* Awarded Silver Star.

George S. Hausen, Chief Yeoman
   San Pedro, Cal.
Samuel O. Hoover, Chief Gunner's Mate
   Center, Ky.
Lewis V. Johnson, Torpedoman, 1st Class
   Summit, Ga.
Paul W. Klaege, Shipfitter, 2nd Class
   Danville, Ill.
Kenneth A. Layton, Chief Radioman
   Brooklyn, N.Y.
Lee Roy Lisk, Chief Commissary Steward
   Albemarle, N.C.
Charles J. Long, Chief Torpedoman
   Miami, Fla.
Edwards M. Morris, Chief Storekeeper
   Philadelphia, Penn.
James T. Murphy, Quartermaster, 1st Class
   Springville, Miss.
Edward A. Olsen, Carpenter's Mate, 1st Class
   Highland Park, Ill.
Donald L. Perkins, Pharmacist's Mate, 1st Class
   Philadelphia, Penn.
Dominador Pigarut, Officers' Cook, 1st Class
   New Orleans, La.
Booker T. Reed, Mess Attendant, 1st Class
   Mobile, Ala.
Wilmer T. Reed, Motor Machinist's Mate, 2nd Class
   Patterson, Mo.
Erwin K. Smith, Metalsmith, 1st Class
   Cleveland, Ohio
Robert E. Smith, Seaman, 1st Class
   Santa Monica, Cal.

CHARLES TUFTS, Chief Boatswain's Mate
  San Pedro, Cal.
EARL W. WALLACE, Chief Carpenter's Mate
  Webster Springs, W.Va.
ARTHUR R. WARNER, Fireman, 1st Class
  Marion, Ohio
HILL C. WHITE, Gunner's Mate, 1st Class
  Austin, Tex.
JOHN P. WICKS, Chief Yeoman
  Fairbury, Neb.
HERBERT S. WING, Chief Torpedoman
  San Diego, Cal.

The following officers and men were later assigned to the squadron:

LIEUTENANT LAWRENCE O. EALY
  Philadelphia, Pa.
LIEUTENANT (JG) SIMEON F. KING
  Birmingham, Ala.
LIEUTENANT RICHARD D. MAHAN
  Newtown Square, Pa.
LIEUTENANT (JG) CHARLES M. MELHORN
  Washington, D.C.
LIEUTENANT (JG) JAMES C. MOUNTCASTLE
  Providence Forge, Va.
LIEUTENANT (JG) SIDNEY RABEKOFF
  New York, N.Y.
* LIEUTENANT ALFRED A. SNOWBALL
  Niles, Ohio

JESSE D. ABBOT	RALPH A. AIELLO
PRENTISS A. ADAMS	ROBERT E. ANDERSON

* Awarded Silver Star.

Francis E. Barnish
Hubert A. Bell
James D. Brown
T. J. Buzbee
Thomas A. Carter
Arthur C. Chambers
Adolph D. Chodkowski
Burgess Clifford, Jr.
William E. Cline
James F. Cook
Clifford Cowley
Walter J. Creed
Robert E. Cruice
Cecil J. Cuthbert
James E. Daniel
Robert J. Dibling
James E. Doehne
Lawrence A. Dorrough
Michael A. Drobny
Ralph D. Elwood
Burney L. Fisk
Andrew C. Garriss
Richard M. Garriss
Lowell L. Hamel
Boyce Hill

Charles W. Jaehnig
Billy B. Kennedy
S. J. Kotarski
Robert E. Leslie
* Thomas S. MacMillan
Donald S. Morey
Guy L. Nichols
Richard J. Nowatzke
John C. Palmer
* Charles A. Pellinat
Glenn H. Penland
Raymond A. Pennel
Donald O. Phelps
Hosey B. Phillips
Eino R. Poteri
John E. Rolfing
Grover T. Scarborough
Clayton W. Stevens
Ollis G. Sweet
Louis E. Tellifson
E. Travis
Robert E. Truitt
Delbert J. Whelan
Wirt C. Williams
Earle M. Witt

* Awarded Silver Star.